11 Work with selections

12 Work with masks

13 Retouch and manipulate

Top 10 Photoshop CS6 Problems Solved

Top 10 Photoshop CS6 tips

Tip 1: How Photoshop, Bridge and Camera Raw work together

Photoshop comes bundled with two helper applications. Adobe Bridge is a separate application that allows you to download and manage images, while the Camera Raw plug-in appears as a dialogue within Photoshop or Bridge. The Mini Bridge panel is an extension of Bridge that resides inside Photoshop and communicates with Bridge. The process of working with an image in Photoshop often involves three stages: a) browsing and selecting images to work with using your computer's operating system, Bridge or Mini Bridge; b) rendering a raw file into an image or pre-editing a rendered image (JPEG or TIFF) in Camera Raw; and c) editing or printing the image with Photoshop.

1 In Bridge:

- Download images from your camera and browse images.
- Browse, search, select and organise images.
- Add metadata.
- Preview images.
- Make slide shows.

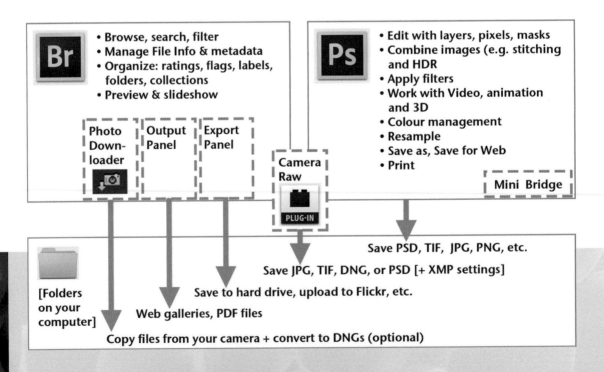

- Make JPEG files with the Save to Disk module in the Export panel.
- Upload images to Facebook, Flickr and Photoshop.com via the Export panel.
- Batch-process files with the image processor: save as JPEG, TIFF or PSD (Photoshop).
- Make web galleries and PDF documents.
- Transfer images to Camera Raw or Photoshop.

2 In Camera Raw:

- Render images from raw camera data.
- Adjust white balance, tone and colour.
- Apply noise reduction.
- Fix chromatic aberrations.
- Add effects such as film grain, vignetting, greyscale conversion and split toning.
- Save files as DNG, JPEG, TIFF and Photoshop files without opening them in Photoshop.
- Transfer images to Photoshop.

3 In Photoshop:

- Use the Mini Bridge panel to preview and to open files.
- Retouch, manipulate and combine images.
- Adjust colour and tone.
- Resample/resize images.
- Add sharpening.
- Edit video and create frame-based (GIF) animation with the Timeline panel.
- Save for Web.
- Save as Photoshop, JPEG, TIFF, PNG, etc.
- Print.

Tip 2: Use Photoshop's keyboard controls

To make Photoshop's operation more efficient, the majority of its tools can be selected by keystrokes. Once you understand the categories of keyboard controls, you'll find yourself using the mouse and menu bar a lot less and getting things done a lot faster. However, Photoshop has so many keyboard commands that it's pretty much impossible to memorise them all. Instead, try to remember just the ones you use the most.

1 **Single letter commands**: tap a key to activate a button in the Toolbar. Examples: the Brush (B), Marquee (M), Crop (C), Type (T), Clone Stamp (S) and Spot Healing Brush (J) tools. You can hover the mouse pointer over a button to see a tool tip with the keyboard shortcut for that button.

2 **Command | Ctrl + letter**: keyboard shortcut to invoke a command from the menu bar. Example: use Command | Ctrl + C to copy and Command | Ctrl + V to paste. Available keyboard shortcuts are shown on the right side of the menus. In many cases, you'll use other modifiers (e.g. Shift and Option | Alt) along with Command | Ctrl to trigger a command.

3 **Command | Ctrl + drag**: most tools (the Brush tool in particular) temporarily convert to the Move tool when you hold down the Command | Ctrl key. If you drag the cursor while holding down the key, you will reposition the current layer unless it is locked (e.g. the Background layer is always locked).

4 **Control-click | Right-click**: displays a contextual menu related to the item that you're clicking on. It's sometimes referred to as 'Context-click'. Examples: Control-click | Right-click on a layer's label for a menu to convert the layer to a smart object. Control-click | Right-click on a layer mask for a menu to open the Mask Options dialogue.

5 **Option | Alt**: invokes an alternative mode for the current tool. Example: Option | Alt temporarily converts the Brush tool into the Eyedropper tool. Option | Alt-click

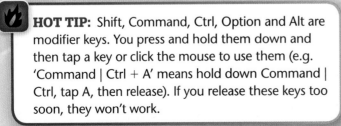

HOT TIP: Shift, Command, Ctrl, Option and Alt are modifier keys. You press and hold them down and then tap a key or click the mouse to use them (e.g. 'Command | Ctrl + A' means hold down Command | Ctrl, tap A, then release). If you release these keys too soon, they won't work.

in the image to sample a colour, then release the key to revert to the Brush tool and continue painting with the new colour.

6 **Shift + letter**: cycle through tools that are grouped under the same button. Example: once you tap M to activate the Marquee tool button, you can tap Shift + M to switch between the Rectangular and Elliptical Marquee tools.

7 **Shift-click**: generally used to select more. Example: in the Layers panel, once you click to select a layer, Shift-click on another layer to select it and any layers in between.

8 **Shift-drag**: constrains movement. (Dragging means holding down the mouse button and then moving the mouse while continuing to hold the button down. You release the mouse button to complete the drag.) Examples: Shift-drag with the brush tool to draw perfectly horizontal or vertical lines. If you Shift-drag with a Marquee tool, you'll make perfect circular or rectangular selections.

ALERT: There are some differences between the modifier keys on the Mac and Windows. When there are differences, we'll show the Windows modifier immediately after the Mac modifier, e.g. Command | Ctrl.

Tip 3: Get files from your camera

There are many ways to get files into your computer from your camera, but while we refer to the process as getting files from your camera, it's actually not a great idea to connect the camera directly to the computer and download that way. A better approach is to use a memory card reader that matches your camera's format (usually Compact Flash or SD, though there are others). You plug the card into the reader, then plug the reader into your computer. Downloading that way will progress faster and won't drain your camera's batteries.

Once you have the card reader connected, you can simply use the Mac Finder or Windows: create a new folder and drag the contents of the media card to the folder. However, Adobe Bridge has a built-in tool called Adobe Photo Downloader, which offers some improvements over the bare-bones approach. It can help you organise the files and apply metadata as it imports.

1 Click the Download icon in the upper left corner of Bridge or select File, Get Photos from Camera from the menu bar.

2 You may see a dialogue asking whether you want Photo Downloader to automatically launch. If you choose No, you can change your mind later (Chapter 1 shows the preference setting to control this). You can also tick the Don't show again box so that you don't have to see the question any more.

3 You can use the Standard dialogue to download all the images from the card or click the Advanced Dialog button for more features.

4 Use the Advanced Dialog if you want the option to tick boxes to select which files to download. You can also apply metadata (e.g. your copyright information) as you import. You can use the Standard Dialog button to switch back at any time.

5 Click the Choose button in either dialogue to specify where you want the files to be saved. Use the Create Subfolder button to determine whether the files are further arranged in subfolders and how those subfolders are named.

 HOT TIP: If you decide to rename your files on import, it's best to extend the existing filename by adding something at the end of the name. You can also tick the option to Preserve Current Filename in XMP when you rename files. However, if you're using metadata effectively, you really don't need to change the name of the file at all.

6 Both dialogues allow you to rename files as they are downloaded.

7 You can tick the box to convert the files to DNG as you download. Once you tick the box, you can also click the Settings button to configure the conversion. (Recommendations: Preserve Raw Image and Embed Original Raw File.)

8 You can use the Save Copies option to back up your originals as you import. Once you tick the box, you can click the Choose button to determine where your backups will be stored.

9 Click Get Media to copy the files onto the specified hard drive.

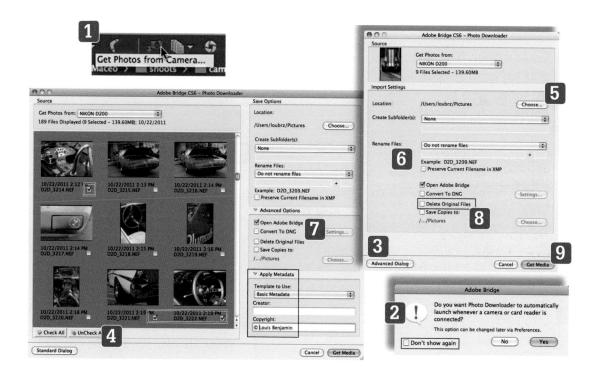

ALERT: The Delete Original Files option in Photo Downloader is not a good idea. You want to check your files after download first to confirm that the transfer was successful. Then you can put the card back into your camera and reformat it.

Tip 4: Enter your copyright with the File Info dialogue

If you don't embed your copyright info as you're importing, you can add it at any time via the File Info dialogue. It's available in both Bridge and Photoshop.

1 Choose File, File Info from the menu bar in Photoshop or Bridge.

2 Click on the Description tab.

3 Enter author, description and keywords (separated by semicolons or commas) as required.

4 Select Copyrighted from the Copyright Status menu.

5 Enter your copyright notice, beginning with the copyright symbol: Option + g on the Mac, Alt + 0169 on Windows.

6 Click OK.

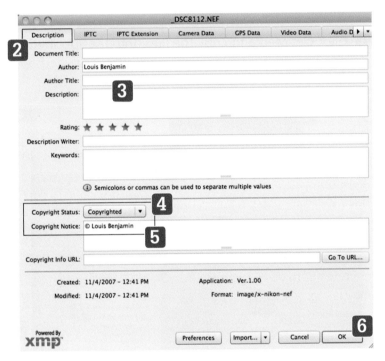

ALERT: Technically, the proper way to write a copyright notice is to either spell out the word or use the symbol, which is a c inside a circle. (c) is not actually recognised as a proper copyright symbol.

? DID YOU KNOW?
These are only some of the items you can embed in your image through the File Info dialogue. The Description, IPTC and IPTC Extension tabs are just three pages of the dialogue that have enterable fields. This is a tool worth becoming familiar with.

 HOT TIP: If you tag or keyword your images in Bridge, that information will also appear when you open them in Photoshop. This info is also embedded into any JPEG or TIFF files you export, making the images identifiable by search engines, including Apple's Spotlight.

Tip 5: Manage location data with the GPS panel

The GPS section of the Metadata panel in Bridge lets you review and edit latitude and longitude data (also known as geotags) embedded in your images. Many websites and apps can use geotags to find images by location or display where an image was shot. Some of the sites with this feature include Flickr, Facebook, Twitter, Picasa Web Albums and Google Panoramio. You can use the panel to add latitude and longitude data to images that do not have them, or to remove geotags when they might pose a potential security risk.

If you're managing and editing photos from your smart phone, chances are they automatically contain geotags as part of their EXIF (camera) metadata. A number of point-and-shoot cameras have the same capability. Most DSLR cameras do not have GPS devices built into them, but a variety of add-on tools can capture your location while you're shooting and add geotags to your images for you.

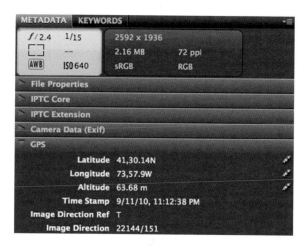

Tip 6: Use noise reduction in Camera Raw

Digital noise tends to be a problem when shooting at high ISO, and it is more pronounced on cameras with smaller sensor chips (e.g. APS or DX). It comes in two forms. Colour noise occurs as bright, coloured dots that appear in a random pattern, particularly in the shadows. Luminance noise is when the pixels are too light or too dark compared with the surrounding pixels. Noise becomes even more of a problem as you try to lighten dark images.

The noise-reduction feature in Camera Raw works very well and is simple to use. Since Camera Raw can edit JPEG and TIFF files as well as raw files, you can use it to remove noise from most images. It also makes the less effective Filter, Noise, Reduce Noise command in Photoshop obsolete.

1 Click on the Detail icon to bring up the sharpening and noise-reduction controls.

2 Zoom in to at least 100% to see the effects of these controls clearly.

3 Use the Luminance slider to even out luminance noise.

4 The Luminance Detail and Luminance Contrast controls become available when you move the Luminance slider above zero. Use them to refine the image further.

5 Use the Color and Color Detail sliders to remove colour noise.

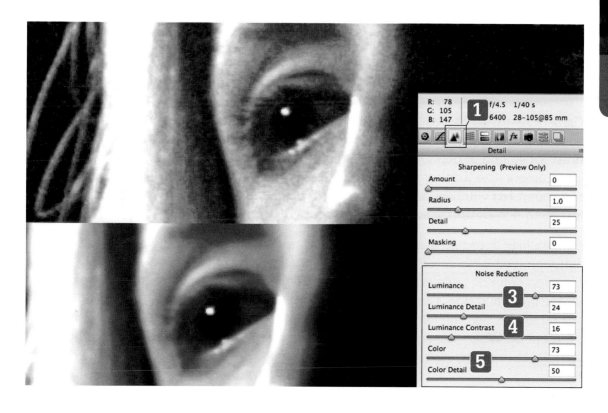

 HOT TIP: Even though there are sharpening controls in Camera Raw, sharpening is usually done in Photoshop at the end of the editing process. The sharpening controls are available under this tab for two reasons. First, a bit of preview sharpening can sometimes help during the adjustment process. Second, it provides a way to sharpen for output when saving files directly from Camera Raw without touching Photoshop.

Tip 7: Edit JPG and TIFF files in Camera Raw

Camera Raw is so named because it was initially designed to process raw files, but it has been able to edit JPEG and TIFF formats for some time. Raw files automatically open for editing in Camera Raw, but you'll use a command to route JPEG or TIFF files into Camera Raw. Editing JPEG and TIFF files in this way does not turn them into raw files, but it lets you take advantage of Camera Raw's interface and most of its features, including non-destructive editing and its superior noise reduction.

Camera Raw does not alter the original JPEG or TIFF image (just as with raw files), although it embeds develop settings inside the file instead of using a separate sidecar file. After you edit a file in Camera Raw, a badge will appear next to its thumbnail in Bridge or Mini Bridge. Double-clicking on the thumbnail of an adjusted JPEG or TIFF will usually reopen the file in Camera Raw, as long as your Camera Raw preferences are set properly. When you return to Camera Raw, you can make additional adjustments, start again or simply revert the file to its original form. You can also discard the develop settings and restore the original version of a file from Bridge.

1. To confirm your Camera Raw preferences in Bridge, select Adobe Bridge CS6, Camera Raw preferences (Windows: Edit, Camera Raw Preferences) or in Photoshop, select Photoshop, Preferences, Camera Raw (Windows: Edit Photoshop, Preferences, Camera Raw) from the menu bar. The JPEG and TIFF handling options will be at the bottom of the dialogue that appears.

2. Confirm that the menus are set to automatically open JPEG and TIFF files with settings. This is the default setting.

3. In Bridge: click to select a thumbnail in the Content panel, then click on the Open in Camera Raw icon in the upper left. Or:

4. In Bridge: Control-click | Right-click a thumbnail and select Open in Camera Raw from the contextual menu.

5 In Mini Bridge, Control-click | Right-click a thumbnail and select Open with, Camera Raw from the contextual menu.

6 After adjusting the image in Camera Raw, click Done to save the develop settings and return to Bridge or click Open Image to save the develop settings and transfer the adjusted image to Photoshop. Notice the badge next to the thumbnail in Bridge.

7 To remove adjustments from an image in Bridge, Control-click | Right-click on the thumbnail and select Develop Settings, Clear Settings from the menu that appears. Or click to select the thumbnail and then select Edit, Develop Settings, Clear Settings from the menu bar.

8 You cannot clear settings directly in Mini Bridge, but you can Control-Click | Right-click on a thumbnail to select Reveal in Bridge from the menu and then follow the previous step to remove the adjustments via Bridge.

ALERT: If JPEG and TIFF file handling are disabled in your Camera Raw preferences, you won't be able to edit those file formats in Camera Raw, even if they have been previously edited in Camera Raw.

HOT TIP: Bear in mind that only Bridge, Camera Raw, Lightroom and Photoshop will recognise any Camera Raw adjustments you've applied to JPEG or TIFF files. If you convert an image to black and white with the HSL/Grayscale panel, its thumbnail and preview will appear in black and white within Bridge, but will remain in colour in the Mac Finder, Windows Explorer, Apple's Preview software and most software that can display images.

WHAT DOES THIS MEAN?

Raw file: even though raw files have a preview that makes them look as though they're images, they are not, and most software cannot read or display them. Raw processing software on your computer is used to translate the camera sensor data in a raw file into an image file (often referred to as rendering). This gives you a wide range of options that is not available when you shoot JPEG or TIFF files with your camera. In that case, the image processor and software built into your camera process the data from the sensor and discard much of it in the process.

Tip 8: Automatically enhance brightness and contrast

You can adjust the tonality of your image by adding a Brightness/Contrast, Levels or Curves adjustment layer. Each has an Auto button that you can use for quick and easy enhancement. In Photoshop CS6, the automatic adjustments for Curves and Levels have been rewritten to make them much more effective. The new auto routines fix a problem that often made things worse by creating colour casts, and also simplify its use. Even though the Auto option works well, you can make further manual adjustments to the settings after clicking the button.

1 Click to select a layer in the Layers panel. The new adjustment layer will be added immediately above the selected layer.

2 Use the Adjustments panel or the menu at the bottom of the Layers panel to add the adjustment layer of your choice (Curves, Levels or Brightness/Contrast).

3 In the Properties panel, click the Auto button.

! ALERT: If you use the Brightness/Contrast adjustment, avoid ticking the box labelled Use Legacy.

HOT TIP: If you're familiar with older versions of Photoshop, you may have learned to Option | Alt-click on the Auto button to display the Auto options dialogue. The new version pretty much does away with the need to do this.

Tip 9: Always embed the colour profile

You'll typically want to edit your master images in either the Adobe RGB or ProPhoto RGB colour space. It's particularly important to embed the colour profile when working with either of these. Many of Photoshop's dialogues that allow you to save an image (e.g. Save As and Save for Web) have an option to embed the colour profile, and several others simply embed the profile without asking. It's best to confirm that the option is ticked when saving, because colour profiles are essential for colour management.

You could say that profiles describe the actual appearance of colours. In essence, a colour profile correlates the RGB colour numbers inside your image with specific real-world colour measurements. Without a colour profile, the RGB numbers inside your image are like a map without a distance key – imagine trying to gauge how large or how far apart things are on a map without one.

Software built into your computer's operating system and within Photoshop can ensure maximum colour fidelity by translating colour numbers in your image to the correct colour numbers for your computer's display and your printer. In the absence of a colour profile, your computer is essentially guessing at what the colours should be and those colours are likely to vary considerably as you move from one computer screen to another or attempt to print what you see onscreen.

You can see in the example that Save for Web has an option to convert to sRGB as you save. When saving files for the Web or email attachments, it's a good idea to convert the copies to sRGB because many web browsers and email applications ignore colour profiles and assume your images are in sRGB. While you might be tempted to simply edit all of your images in sRGB, that's not a good idea because it discards colours that you might want to be able to print.

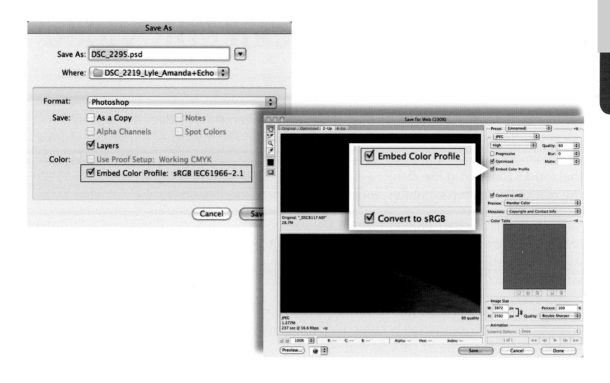

WHAT DOES THIS MEAN?

Why use RGB numbers? The big benefits of using RGB numbers to designate the colours in a digital image are compactness and speed. The precision of colour profiles is key for processes like printing, but it's less critical in many other cases. Adding the colour profile to an image file makes it slightly larger, and colour management requires extra computing power, which could make displaying images unacceptably slow in some situations. For example, smart phones and even the screens on the back of most digital cameras do not use colour management and their colour capability, using simple RGB numbers without the processing overhead of colour management is good enough for most applications.

Tip 10: Now you can edit video in Photoshop

Now that many digital SLRs and even smart phones can shoot video, it seems like a good idea to add the ability to edit video from within Photoshop CS6. Happily, Adobe didn't simply graft an application such as Premiere Elements into a walled-off dialogue that works something like Camera Raw. Instead, video editing is tightly integrated with the rest of Photoshop's features, including 3D.

Video is simply another type of layer in Photoshop. You can apply filters, use adjustment layers, add type and convert type and other flat artwork to 3D in the same manner as you do with still images. You can even animate text and 3D objects. In addition to the visual elements, you can add and edit audio tracks.

You arrange your video in the Timeline panel, which can also handle frame-based animation. When your video is complete, you can render (export) the final product in H.264 MP4, Quicktime or DPX format.

The illustration shows the following:

1 Timeline, including video, 3D text and an audio track.

2 A fade-out has been applied to the 3D text layer.

3 The Layers panel, with a Curves adjustment layer selected. (The Curves controls appear in the Properties panel in the background.)

1 Getting started with Adobe Photoshop CS6

Introduction

In this chapter, we'll look at some key elements of the Adobe Photoshop interface and cover some initial setup.

It is worth noting immediately that even though we talk in terms of 'editing in Photoshop', the process often entails workflows that may involve visiting two support applications – Adobe Bridge and Adobe Camera Raw. This book is arranged to reflect the ways that you might typically use Photoshop, Bridge and Camera Raw with photographic images.

The aim of this book is to provide you with a solid foundation of best practices for working with Photoshop. As you explore and learn about Photoshop, you will quickly discover that there are lots of ways to do the same thing, and you will also find out about features and techniques not covered in this book. Most of the more advanced Photoshop techniques that you will encounter are founded on the basics covered here. So, let's begin ...

Reset Photoshop and Bridge preferences to the default settings

Because Photoshop and Bridge are highly configurable, it can be very confusing to start trying to use these applications with the workspaces rearranged and preferences set to work in a completely different manner than the defaults. In rare cases, your preferences file can become damaged and cause Photoshop to behave strangely. Resetting all of your preferences in one shot will get you back to a familiar configuration. From there, you can recustomise settings as you like.

To reset all your preferences for Photoshop or Bridge to the default settings, do the following:

1 Quit the application.

2 Hold down Shift + Option | Alt + Command | Ctrl and restart the application.

3 Continue holding the keys until you see a dialogue box asking what you'd like to do.

4 For Photoshop, click Yes.

5 For Bridge, tick the box marked Reset Preferences. You also have the option of purging the thumbnail cache. (If in doubt, don't purge.) Then click OK.

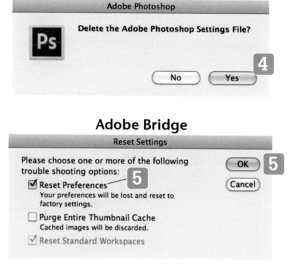

HOT TIP: This feature is probably most useful in situations such as schools, where lots of people might use the same machine and configure Photoshop to their own preferences. Once you reset the preferences to their defaults, you can work in a familiar environment by adjusting a few key settings under the Photoshop, Preferences menu and select your colour management policies under the Edit, Color Settings dialogue.

Adjust Photoshop preferences

In this section, we'll look at the preferences found under the Photoshop menu (the Edit menu on Windows). Some recommended settings are given below and more are listed in the next section. Shortly, we'll look at two other sets of preferences: Color Settings (for colour management) and Workspaces (preferences that manage the arrangement of your panels).

The keystroke to open the General preferences page is Command | Ctrl + K. Click the words in the box at the left side of the dialogue to navigate between preference pages, i.e. General, Interface, File Handling, etc. You can adjust settings on multiple pages before clicking OK, which saves all settings and closes the dialogue. Clicking Cancel discards all changes and closes the dialogue.

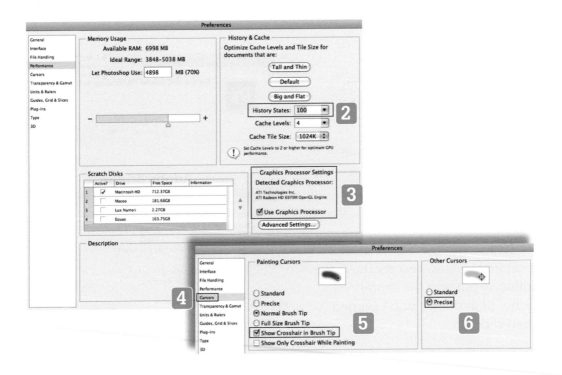

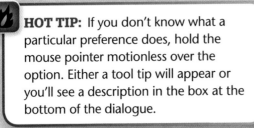

HOT TIP: If you don't know what a particular preference does, hold the mouse pointer motionless over the option. Either a tool tip will appear or you'll see a description in the box at the bottom of the dialogue.

1. Select Photoshop, Preferences, Performance (Windows: Edit, Preferences, Performance) from the menu bar to go directly to the Performance page.

2. In the History & Cache section, increase the number of history states to somewhere between 50 and 100. Setting Photoshop to remember too many history states can slow down your machine, but setting too few can limit your ability to undo mistakes.

3. In the Graphics Processor Settings section of the Performance page, the preference labelled Use Graphics Processor should be ticked. If you are not able to tick it, your computer does not support the feature. (See the alert box below for details.)

4. Click Cursors on the left side of the dialogue to switch to that page.

5. In the Painting Cursors section, make sure that Normal Brush Tip is selected and that Show Crosshair in Brush Tip is ticked. This allows you to know exactly where the centre of a brush is, especially when working with larger brushes. Normal Brush Tip shows the outline of the brush at the point where soft brushes (hardness less than 100%) reach 50% density. That means part of the brush extends outside the circle and you can paint with that part of the brush to achieve subtle effects.

6. Select Precise in the Other Cursors section.

ALERT: Photoshop relies on features built into more advanced graphics cards from ATI and NVIDEA. While one of these cards is likely to be built into most computers sold in the past three years or so, you won't be able to use some Photoshop features if your computer does not have one of the more advanced graphics cards.

Set recommended Photoshop preferences

Each of the preferences pages has a number of optional settings that are worthy of some discussion. Since the last section left off in the Cursors page, we'll begin there.

1 Cursors page: Show only Crosshair While Painting – you usually don't want this, but it can boost performance with large brushes. Turn it on only when you need to.

2 General page:
- Note the button marked Reset All Warning Dialogs on this page. It restores any dialogues that you might have turned off by ticking the box marked Don't Show Again.
- You can set the HUD Color Picker to one of the Hue Wheel options. While the default Hue Strip interface emulates Photoshop's standard colour picker, the Hue Wheel displays colour relationships more clearly.

3 Performance page: Cache levels and Tile Size – use the default, unless you have a special reason to adjust this.

4 Guides, Grid & Slices page: change the style of the grid and adjust the spacing and subdivisions of the grid as needed.

5 Type page: as you type, Use Smart Quotes instantly converts the double quote keystroke to the appropriate opening or closing curly quote. If you need to enter a plain double quote (to specify inches, for example), you can untick this option and make your mark, then turn it back on.

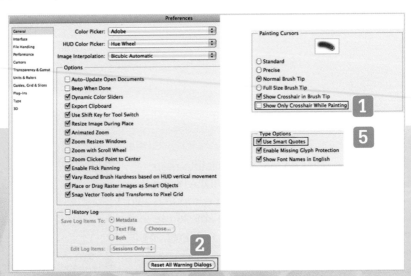

Edit and save colour settings

An important aspect of working with photographs is maintaining accurate colour. By setting a working colour space and establishing policies on how to handle conflicting or missing colour information, you can be assured of accurate colour whether you are printing an image or preparing to post it on the Internet.

1. From the Edit menu, choose Color Settings (Shortcut: Shift + Command | Ctrl + K).

2. From the Settings menu at the top of the dialogue box, choose Europe Prepress 3.

3. In the Working Spaces section locate the Gray menu, and change it to Gray Gamma 2.2. (This will change options in the menus below and the Settings menu will now say Custom.)

4. Leave the Color Management Policies set to preserve the embedded profiles and to ask in case of profile mismatches or missing profiles.

5. Click Save.

6. In the Save As box, enter a meaningful name such as General Photo. If you are using a copy of Photoshop on a shared computer, it is a good idea to include your initials in the name of the preference set.

7. Click Save.

8. When the Color Settings Comment box appears, you must click OK to finish saving the settings. Do not click the Cancel button.

9. Click OK to exit the colour settings dialogue.

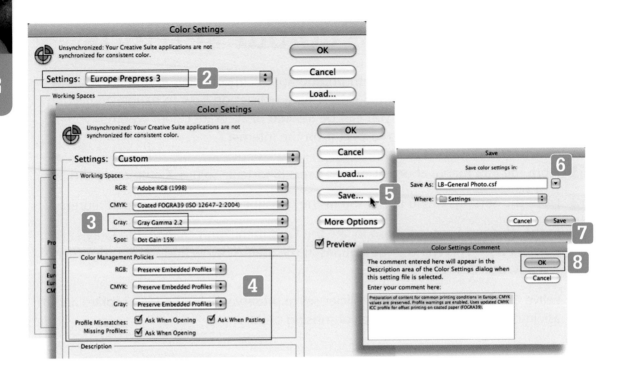

Select a colour theme in Photoshop and Bridge

Adobe created the new dark interface options for CS6 in part because the colour of the interface affects the appearance of colours and tones in your image. If the interface is too dark, too light or not neutral in colour, it can adversely affect your editing. The default theme is an improvement over the colour schemes used in earlier versions of Photoshop.

The colour themes from dark to light are known as 'pumpernickel', 'dark rye' (the default), 'whole wheat' and 'sourdough'. The 'whole wheat' theme resembles the colour palette of earlier versions of Photoshop.

1 In Photoshop, Select Photoshop, Preferences, Interface from the menu bar.

2 Click one of the Color Theme swatches to change the interface colour.

3 Change the Full Screen colour menu to Dark Gray (instead of Black).

4 Click OK to exit the dialogue.

5 To change the colour of the 'pasteboard' (the neutral area surrounding your image), Control-click | Right-click outside the image area to reveal a menu and select a colour from the menu. Recommended: Medium or Dark Gray.

6 In Bridge, select Adobe Bridge CS6, Preferences from the menu bar.

7 Click one of the Color Theme swatches or use the User Interface Brightness slider to change the overall colour.

8 Use the Image Backdrop slider to change the brightness of the colour behind the Content and Preview panels.

9 Optional: use the Accent Color menu to customise the way items are highlighted when you select them.

10 Click OK to exit the dialogue.

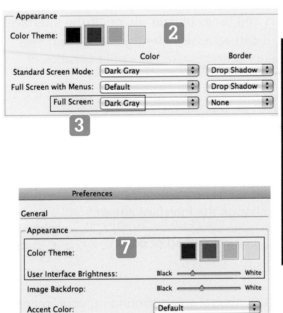

Set up Bridge preferences

In the previous section, we looked at the options to adjust the colour scheme of Adobe Bridge. We'll look at a few more optional preferences here. The labelling system in Bridge can be a useful organisational tool. Rather than use the default descriptions, you can assign different names to the coloured labels. You can also set Bridge to automatically start the Photo Downloader utility whenever you connect a card reader or a camera to your computer.

1 Select Adobe Bridge CS6, Preferences (Windows: Edit, Preferences) to open the General page of the Preferences dialogue.

2 To automatically open Photo Downloader when a camera is connected, tick the box in the Behavior section.

3 Click Labels in the box on the left side of the dialogue to manage labelling.

4 Click Thumbnails on the left side of the dialogue to switch to that page. Tick the box at the bottom of the dialogue marked Show Tooltips to reveal useful info about thumbnails when you hover the cursor over them.

General Page:

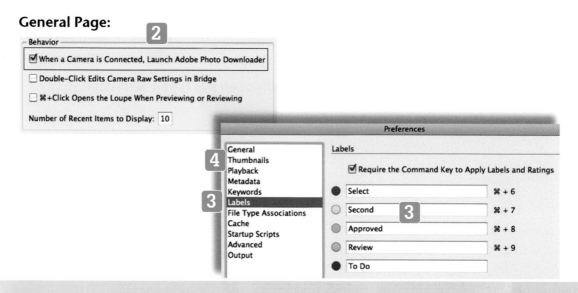

HOT TIP: By default, double-clicking a raw file in Bridge passes the file to Photoshop, which then opens the raw file in its copy of Camera Raw. That means Photoshop will be tied up until you finish working in Camera Raw. Instead, you can tell Bridge to open the file with its own copy of Camera Raw and free up Photoshop. On the General page, tick the box labelled Double-Click Edits Camera Raw Settings in Bridge.

Set preferences for Adobe Camera Raw

Camera Raw is a plug-in, meaning there is no separate application to launch. It is available as an on-demand resource inside both Photoshop and Bridge. You can adjust your Camera Raw preferences from either Photoshop or Bridge. Advanced users may have specific reasons to diverge from the settings recommended below, but these general-purpose settings will suit a wide range of uses.

1. In Photoshop: select Photoshop, Preferences, Camera Raw (Windows: Edit, Preferences, Camera Raw).

2. In Bridge: select Adobe Bridge CS6, Camera Raw Preferences (Windows: Edit, Camera Raw Preferences).

3. In the General section of the dialogue, set Apply sharpening to Preview images only and set Save image settings in to Sidecar ".xmp" files.

4. If you choose to work with the DNG format, make sure you tick Ignore sidecar ".xmp" files. That's what tells Camera Raw to store the adjustments in the DNG file.

5. In the Default Image Settings section, it's best to tick only the box marked Apply auto grayscale mix when converting to grayscale.

6. Set the JPEG and TIFF menus to Automatically open [file type]s with settings.

7. Click OK to save the settings.

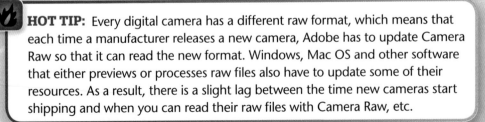

HOT TIP: Every digital camera has a different raw format, which means that each time a manufacturer releases a new camera, Adobe has to update Camera Raw so that it can read the new format. Windows, Mac OS and other software that either previews or processes raw files also have to update some of their resources. As a result, there is a slight lag between the time new cameras start shipping and when you can read their raw files with Camera Raw, etc.

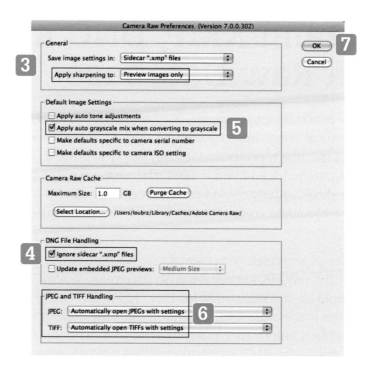

Understand XMP, DNG and the Camera Raw Database

When Camera Raw processes an image file, it essentially builds a recipe for how to transform the original image into the edited preview that you see on screen. It keeps the original file intact, protecting it from being degraded, which is what non-destructive (or parametric) editing means. The recipe (i.e. the develop settings and adjustment data) is stored separately in one of three ways: as an XMP file (the default method), within the metadata compartment of a DNG file or in the Camera Raw Database.

XMP or 'sidecar' files sit alongside the original raw file. The name of the sidecar file matches that of the raw file, except it has an extension of XMP. For example, DSC_1234.XMP would be the sidecar file for DSC_1234.NEF – a raw file from a Nikon camera. (Most Canon models use CR2; extensions vary by make and model.) Whenever you begin editing a file, Camera Raw looks for settings in its companion XMP file in the same folder. If you delete the XMP, move the raw file onto a new folder or disc without its XMP, or change the name of one of the files so they no longer match, Camera Raw will treat the raw file as if it had never been edited. The implication is that when you copy or move raw files, it is important to copy or move the matching XMP files along with them.

DNG (Adobe Digital Negative) files combine the original raw file and the sidecar file into a single document, eliminating the need for an XMP file – when you copy or move a DNG file, everything goes along with it. The DNG format is a published standard, which offers some archival benefits and other features worth reading about. The downside is that converting your raw files to DNG adds more steps to your workflow. See www.adobe.com/products/dng/ for more information.

The Camera Raw Database is a special file that is stored in a single central location on your computer. It captures internal data from any raw files that you edit and keeps track of them. Even if you rename a file, Camera Raw will find and apply the appropriate edits as necessary.

? DID YOU KNOW?

When you use the Database option, there are normally no XMP files, but you can export XMPs when you need them.

1. To export DNG files from Camera Raw, click the Save Image button in the lower left corner of the dialogue (see Chapter 3). In the Save Options dialogue, set the File Extension to .dng and the Format to Digital Negative. All other settings are optional, though Use Lossy Compression is not recommended.

2. You can also convert your raw files to DNGs as you import them with Photo Downloader: tick the box marked Convert to DNG in the main dialogue. Click the Settings button to adjust the conversion settings. Preserve Raw Image and Embed Original Raw File are recommended.

3. To use the Camera Raw database option, select Camera Raw Preferences from the Adobe Bridge CS6 or Photoshop menu (Windows: Edit, Camera Raw Preferences), then select Camera Raw database from the menu at the top of the Camera Raw Preferences dialogue.

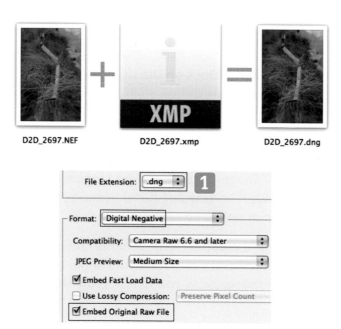

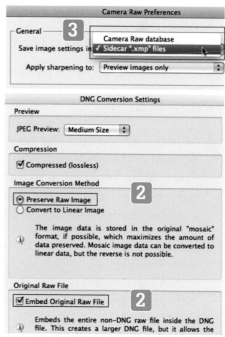

Understand Photoshop's layout

Photoshop's rich functionality is controlled through a potentially overwhelming array of panels, dialogues and menus. Once you understand how the various elements work, you'll find it much easier to get around and get things done.

1 Tools panel and Options bar: you're likely to work quite a bit with the tools on the vertical panel on the left side of the screen, such as the Brush tool, Healing Brush, Clone Stamp, Marquee and Lasso tools. Whenever you select a tool in the Tools panel, its controls appear in the Options bar along the top of the work area.

2 Document tabs: a row of tabs immediately beneath the Options bar allows you to work with multiple documents. Click a tab to display the document.

3 Layers and Properties panels: in Photoshop, images consist of one or more layers, which you create and organise via the Layers panel. Adjustment layers and 3D layers have parameters that can be edited via the Properties panel (e.g. the Curves controls shown), which is new in Photoshop CS6.

4 Utility panels: you'll find a number of panels in the Dock on the right side of the Photoshop environment. They allow you to select brush tips, stylise text and work with masks, channels, paths, 3D, etc.

5 Mini Bridge and Timeline panels: these panels are located in their own dock at the bottom of the work area. The dock can be collapsed to take up very little room. You can use Mini Bridge to open or preview images, drag and drop files into your compositions, and present ad-hoc slide shows. The Timeline panel allows you to edit video or create frame-based animation such as animated GIF files.

6 Workspaces: the Workspace menu appears in the upper right corner of the work area. It allows you to quickly switch between different arrangements of panels. Panels can crowd out your image, and workspaces allow you to efficiently show, hide and rearrange them as needed.

7 Keyboard shortcuts and Menu commands: many items in Photoshop's menus show keyboard shortcuts that you can invoke with the Command | Ctrl key. There are so many that it's best to memorise only your favourite ones. In addition, you can activate the Tools panel buttons by tapping a letter key without the Command | Ctrl key. The modifier keys (Shift, Option | Alt) allow you to invoke special modes for some tools, and Control-click | Right-click brings up contextual menus.

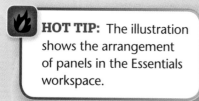

HOT TIP: The illustration shows the arrangement of panels in the Essentials workspace.

Use the Layers and Properties panels

Layers are fundamental components of images inside Photoshop and you'll probably use the Layers panel more than any other interface. When you open most images for the first time, the Layers panel will contain only a Background layer. As you edit an image, you're likely to add or duplicate a layer before using almost any of Photoshop's other tools, commands or filters. You'll use the panel to stack additional layers as needed and control which ones are visible.

When you click on an adjustment layer or layer mask, its corresponding controls will appear in the Properties panel. In the illustration, a Black & White adjustment layer is selected and its controls appear in the Properties panel.

1 Add adjustment layer menu.

2 Add pixel layer.

3 Add layer mask.

4 Set blending mode and opacity.

5 Toggle layer visibility.

6 Filter layers.

7 Select layer or mask settings.

DID YOU KNOW?
Photoshop can create several kinds of layers, including pixel, adjustment, fill, type (text), 3D and video.

HOT TIP: The two panels are shown side by side in the illustration, but their arrangement will depend upon how your workspace is configured.

Use the Tools panel and Options bar

Photoshop's tools are organised in a vertical panel on the left side of the work area.

1 You can hover the mouse pointer over any of the buttons to see a tool tip containing the name of the tool and its keyboard shortcut.

2 To activate a button, click on it or tap its shortcut key. The button will darken to show that it is active. (In this example, the rectangular marquee tool is active.)

3 Many of the buttons have a small triangle in the lower right corner to indicate that they house multiple related tools. To display the tools grouped within a button, place the cursor over the button and hold down the mouse button. A menu will appear with a small square next to the current tool.

4 You can select a new tool from the menu or you can use a keyboard shortcut to cycle through the nested tools. Hold down the Shift key and tap the button's keyboard shortcut repeatedly until the desired tool becomes active (e.g. tapping Shift + J lets you select among the Spot Healing Brush, Healing Brush, Patch, Content-Aware Move and Red Eye tools).

5 The Options bar sits immediately above the Tools panel and extends horizontally to the right. Whenever you activate a tool, the Options bar updates to show the controls for the current tool. (In this example, the Red Eye tool options are displayed.)

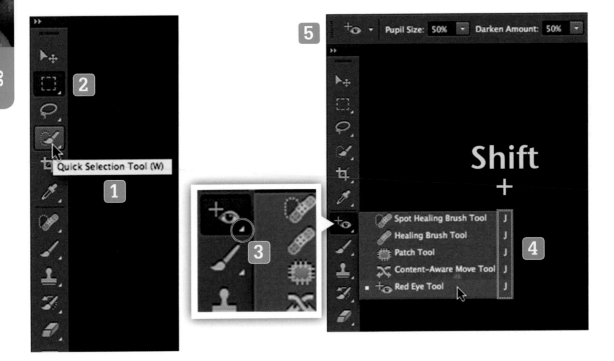

Quick Selection Tool (W)

5 Pupil Size: 50% ▾ Darken Amount: 50% ▾

Shift
+

Spot Healing Brush Tool   J
Healing Brush Tool   J
Patch Tool   J   **4**
Content-Aware Move Tool   J
Red Eye Tool   J

ALERT: You use a letter key without the Command | Ctrl key to select an item from the Tools panel. Command | Ctrl plus a letter key invokes a command from the menu bar.

Use utility panels and the Window menu

Photoshop provides more than 20 panels beyond the Tools, Layers and Properties panels to facilitate your work. Some are described below.

1 Brush, Brush Presets, Tool Presets: these panels allow you to select and manage the many variations of brushes available to you. You can build a brush on the fly with the Brush panel and then save it as a Brush Preset. You can also combine a Brush Preset with a foreground colour and save it as a Tool Preset.

2 Color, Swatches and Styles: both the Color and Swatches panels provide ways to quickly select colours to work with. You can use Styles to apply drop shadows and other effects to layers.

3 Character, Character Styles, Paragraph, Paragraph Styles: with these panels, you can manage typography and even use style sheets with your text.

4 Masks: you can use masks with layers and groups to define what parts of the layer or group are visible or where an adjustment is applied within the image. Through the Masks panel, you can control the density of a mask and use the feather setting to soften tonal transitions in the mask. You can also use the panel to select colours within the image to define the mask, refine edges within the mask or invert it.

5 3D: use the panel to create and edit 3D objects.

6 Timeline: use the panel to import and edit video or frame-based animation.

7 Because panels can take up valuable screen space, they can be rearranged and even hidden (closed) to keep your work area uncluttered. All panels have a menu icon in the upper right corner that you can click to reveal a fly-out menu. It includes options specific to the panel along with a Close command that will hide the panel.

 HOT TIP: The 3D features are only available in Photoshop CS6 Extended. If you're running the Standard edition, you won't see them.

Use workspaces

The Workspace menu is located in the upper right corner of Photoshop. You can use it to quickly switch between different arrangements of panels – Photoshop will show, hide and reorganise them for you. This is handy because many of Photoshop's utility panels can take up valuable screen space and are useful for only certain types of work. There are pre-defined workspaces for photography, typography, painting, motion (video and animation) and 3D. You can use the pre-defined workspaces as-is, or modify them and save your own.

Whenever a workspace is active, Photoshop tracks any changes you make to it. That way, you don't have to re-save the workspace whenever you rearrange it. To restore the arrangement to the way it was when it was first defined, you use the Reset [Workspace] command. In the illustration, you can see the default Essentials and Photography workspaces. A third workspace is being created by rearranging and adding panels to the Photography workspace. The steps below outline how you can create a custom workspace from the default Photography workspace.

1 Select Photography from the Workspace menu.

2 Use the fly-out menu in the upper right corner of the panels to close any panels you want to remove from the workspace.

3 Use the Window menu to reveal any additional panels you might like to include in the new workspace.

4 Drag panels to rearrange them. (Note the blue highlight in the middle of the illustration – a panel is snapping into place.)

5 When you are satisfied with the workspace arrangement, choose New Workspace from the Workspace menu.

6 Enter a name (e.g. Simple Steps) and click Save. The new workspace name will be selected in the menu.

7 To return the Photography workspace to its original arrangement, first select Photography from the Workspace menu and then select Reset Photography from the same menu.

 HOT TIP: The Workspace menu is duplicated in the menu bar. You can find it under Window, Workspace.

2 Browse, manage and show images with Adobe Bridge

Introduction

In this chapter, we're going to look at how Bridge provides browsing, management and presentation services for Photoshop and other Creative Suite applications. We'll also look at how Bridge and Photoshop collaborate, in terms of switching between the two applications, via the Mini Bridge panel in Photoshop.

The Bridge application can present slide shows, make web galleries and export PDF files easily, and Photoshop automation features in Bridge allow you to batch-process images.

Mini Bridge is a light version of Adobe Bridge in the form of a Photoshop panel, which uses Bridge as a processing engine – Bridge runs in the background, providing resources to Mini Bridge so that it doesn't tax Photoshop. For example, Bridge does the work of creating thumbnails and keeping files synchronised. Mini Bridge makes browsing for files (especially when combining multiple files into a single Photoshop document) more streamlined. When you need the full features of Bridge, Mini Bridge makes it easy to take your current selection of images with you as you switch to and from Bridge.

Bridge can also process and save files via its Export panel, Output module and Tools menu commands. We'll cover those topics in Chapters 5 and 17.

Use key elements of Bridge

This section will briefly cover some of the more salient features of Bridge. The Bridge workspace is divided into five main areas, consisting of three vertical columns that contain panels, a header and a footer.

1 Use the Folders panel to navigate the files and folders on your computer. When you select a folder, its contents appear as thumbnails inside the Content panel.

2 The Collections panel contains what are essentially virtual folders – you click on a collection to display its thumbnails in the Content panel. The difference is that you can drag files from multiple drives and folders into a collection.

3 The Content panel displays thumbnails for the files and folders within the currently selected folder, collection or search results. Buttons at the lower right corner of the Bridge window allow you to change the Content panel view and a slider allows you to resize the thumbnails.

4 The Metadata and Keywords panels allow you to view and manage descriptive data attached to your files.

5 Use the Filter panel to refine the selection of thumbnails appearing in the Content panel based on keywords, star ratings, labels or even metadata from your camera (e.g. the focal length or shutter speed).

6 The left side of the header contains navigation tools and the boomerang button, which switches you back to Photoshop. There are also buttons for Photo Downloader, opening the selected images in Camera Raw, and switching to the Output module.

7 The right side of the header includes the Workspace Switcher and the Search box. You can rearrange panels (drag them by their tabs) and save your own workspaces, too.

8 You can size the preview panel to show a lot of detail, or hide it completely. When you click in the preview image, the Loupe tool will magnify the area around the point that you clicked. Click inside the Loupe to put it away.

HOT TIP: Bridge can only browse media on volumes that are connected to the computer. When you disconnect from that network server or eject that disk, its thumbnails and previews go away. This is different from a cataloguing tool such as Lightroom, which gathers up thumbnails and previews of the disks it scans and stores them in an image database. When you disconnect the disk from your computer, Lightroom can still browse the information in its database.

Navigate with folders and favourites

In most of the standard workspaces in Bridge, the Favorites and Folders panels are grouped together on the left side. The example here shows them as they appear in the Essentials workspace. To reveal a panel, simply click its tab.

1 Click on an icon in the Folders panel to display its contents as thumbnails in the Content panel.

2 In the Folders panel, click the triangle to the left of a folder icon to expand or collapse its subfolders.

3 You can also double-click on folder icons in the Content panel to drill down into subfolders. The Folder panel selection will update accordingly.

4 To add a favourite, Control-click | Right-click on any folder or drive in the Folders panel or any thumbnail in the Content panel to display a contextual menu and then select Add to Favorites.

5 When the Favorites panel is visible, you can create new favourites by dragging items into it from the Content panel.

6 In the Favorites panel, click on an item to browse that location in the Content panel.

7 To remove a favourite, Control-click | Right-click on an item in the Favorites panel to display a menu and select Remove from Favorites.

8 Click on the triangle in the upper left corner of the Bridge window to reveal the Parents and Favorites menu. Select an item to navigate to that location.

9 Use the Go Back | Go Forward arrows or select an item from the Recent Files and Folders menu to re-visit recently browsed locations.

10 Click the Boomerang button to switch to Photoshop. Mini Bridge will update to match the Content panel of Bridge.

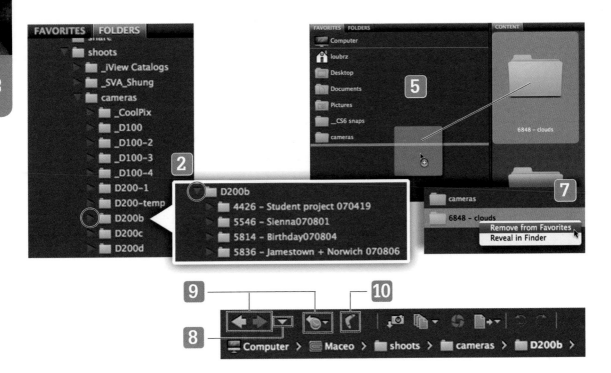

Browse and select images in the Content panel

The Content panel displays thumbnails for the files and folders within a folder, collection or the results of a search. When browsing collections, the upper right corner of the panel includes a button to remove images from the collection. The location and size of the Content panel will depend on how your workspace is configured. Bridge comes with several ready-made workspaces (Essentials, Filmstrip, Output, etc.) and you can create your own. In this example, the Essentials workspace was modified – the Collections panel was moved up and grouped with Favorites and Folders. The bottom of the Preview panel was pulled downwards to expand it.

1. Click on a thumbnail to view it in the Preview panel.

2. Click in the Preview panel to activate the Loupe tool. (There may be a slight delay while the tool starts up.) Click in the image or drag the Loupe to view different parts of the preview.

3. Click on the Loupe again to put it away.

4. The lower right corner of the Bridge window contains buttons to change the format of the Content panel and a slider to control the size of the thumbnails.

5. To rotate images, click on the image and then click the Rotate icons in the upper left corner of the Bridge window. You can also use Command | Ctrl + [to rotate counter-clockwise and Command | Ctrl +] to rotate clockwise.

6. Drag images to sort manually, or use the Sort menu.

7. To select more than one image, click the first thumbnail, then Shift-click on another to select it and all images between, or Command | Control-click to individually select additional images. You can also Command | Control-click to deselect individual images after you have selected a group of them.

8 The Preview panel shows multiple images when you select a group.

9 With one or more images selected, hit the space bar for a full-screen preview. You can switch between full-screen images with the arrow keys. Hit the space bar again to exit full screen.

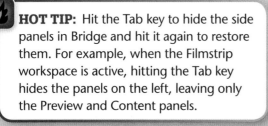

HOT TIP: Hit the Tab key to hide the side panels in Bridge and hit it again to restore them. For example, when the Filmstrip workspace is active, hitting the Tab key hides the panels on the left, leaving only the Preview and Content panels.

Use workspaces

You can easily rearrange Bridge to suit your needs – sometimes, for instance, you may want a big preview panel and at other times, you may need a lot of thumbnails. Workspaces allow you to switch between different arrangements with the click of a button. Whenever you create a useful arrangement, you can save a custom workspace.

The Workspace Switcher in the upper right corner of the Bridge window consists of a configurable row of text buttons showing the names of several workspaces and a triangle that houses the Workspace Switcher menu. Workspaces are 'live', which means that Bridge will automatically remember the new layout of a workspace whenever you rearrange it, but you can easily reset any workspace to its original layout.

1 To activate a workspace, click a button in the Workspace Switcher or select one from its menu. You can also use a keyboard shortcut for the first six workspaces. Their shortcut keys appear in the menu.

2 Drag the vertical bars at the left edge of the button group to expand or shrink the row of buttons. You can also drag buttons to reorder them.

3 Drag panels by their tabs to rearrange a workspace. Blue highlights will appear to indicate where the panel will snap to if you release the mouse button at a given point. A blue box indicates that the panel will be grouped with the outlined panel(s) and a horizontal line indicates that the panel will snap between, above or below other panels.

4 To create a custom workspace, select New Workspace from the Workspace Switcher menu. A dialogue with some options will appear. After you click Save, Bridge will add your new workspace to the button bar and select it.

5 To reset workspaces to their original arrangement, choose Reset Workspace from the Workspace Switcher menu to revert the current workspace, or choose Reset Standard Workspaces to reset all the standard workspaces at once.

6 To delete any of your custom workspaces, choose Delete Workspace from the Workspace Switcher Menu and then select a workspace from the menu in the dialogue that appears. Click Delete to remove the workspace.

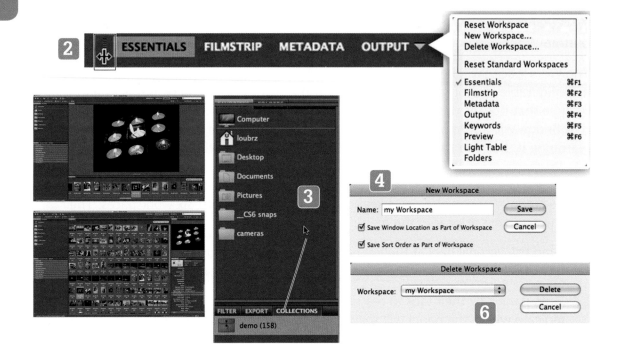

HOT TIP: If you rearrange an existing workspace (e.g. Essentials) and then save a new custom workspace, the two workspaces will be the same at first. You can reset the first workspace to return it to its original configuration.

Apply ratings, labels, keywords and IPTC metadata

You can embed a wealth of information into your image using IPTC data. Select one or more files, and then use the Metadata panel or the File Info dialogue to apply your metadata as required. The Metadata panel and File Info dialogues both have keyword fields. You can type your keywords directly into those fields, separated by either commas or semicolons. Once the metadata are added, you can search for and filter files based upon that data.

1 Select one or more thumbnails.

2 Use the Label menu (in the menu bar) or keyboard shortcuts to apply star ratings and labels.

3 In the Metadata panel, click in the fields with pencil icons to enter data. When you've finished, click the tick mark icon at the bottom of the panel to apply.

4 Select File, File Info from the menu bar to open the File Info dialogue.

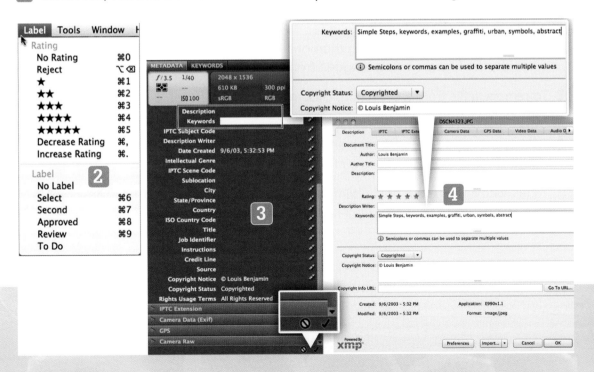

Use organisation features: collections and filters

Favourites and folder browsing are very useful, but they can only show you files from a single folder at a time. Collections allow you to work with groups of images that span multiple folders or drives. They are essentially virtual folders that allow you to drag files from any folder and drop them in. The collection simply keeps a reference to the file instead of making a copy. Whenever you browse a folder or collection, Bridge will compile a list of metadata from the images in the Content panel and display it in the Filter panel. You can tick items in the Filter panel to control which thumbnails are visible in the Content panel.

1. To create a new collection, click the New Collection button at the bottom of the Collections panel. If any files are selected in the Content panel, you will be asked whether you want to include them. Enter a name for the collection and hit the Return/Enter key to accept.

2. After creating a collection, Bridge will select the collection and display it in the Content panel. You can click the Go Back arrow (upper left corner of Bridge) to return to the previous selection.

3. To add files to a collection, drag thumbnails into it from the Content panel. (In the example, the files are being dragged from another collection.)

4. To remove a file from a collection, click in the Content panel to select it and then click Remove from Collection.

5. To delete a collection, click on it and then click on the trashcan icon in the lower right corner of the Collections panel.

6. To activate a filter, click on an item in the Filter panel. A tick mark will appear next to it.

7 To combine filters, click to tick more items.

8 To cancel a filter, click on it again. The tick mark will clear.

Present a slide show

The Slideshow feature is a convenient way to put together an ad-hoc presentation of images from your Content panel. You can browse a folder or collection and use the Filter panel to make an initial selection for your slide show. If none of the files in the Content panel is selected, Slideshow will display all the files in your Content panel. Otherwise, you can select one and then use Shift-click or Command | Control-click to select more files to show. If you want to present the slide show more than once, you can gather the selected files into a new collection. You can also drag files to sequence your slide show. Once you have your files selected and sequenced, do the following:

1 Select View, Slideshow Options from the menu bar.

2 Set your desired preferences. (N.B. The Repeat Slideshow option loops the slide show continuously.)

3 Click Play to start the slide show.

4 Hit the Space bar to pause or resume.

5 Hit Esc to end the slide show.

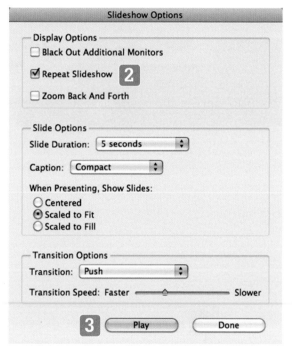

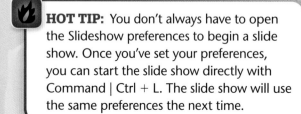

Use Mini Bridge

You'll find the Mini Bridge panel in the Dock at the bottom of the Photoshop window in the Essentials, Photography and Motion workspaces, or you can reveal it in any workspace by choosing Window, Extension, Mini Bridge from the menu bar. You can think of it as a 'light' version of Bridge that's actually powered by Bridge. With Mini Bridge, you can browse, search, select, open and process files from within Photoshop instead of switching to Bridge. One significant differentiation is that the Navigation pod and thumbnail display in Mini Bridge work differently from the Folders and Content panels in Bridge. Mini Bridge cannot display folders and aliases (shortcuts) and the Navigation pod does not have disclosure triangles that you can click to expand the contents of folders. The Navigation pod does offer an alternative approach to navigating through folders, but you'll have to switch back to Bridge to work with aliases.

1. If Bridge is not running when you activate Mini Bridge, you can click a button to start it. As soon as Bridge is online, the panel will update.

2. The Tool bar occupies a narrow strip along the top of the panel. It houses the navigation arrows, switch to Bridge button, View menu, Sort menu and Path bar on the left. The Filter menu and search field are on the right. You can hide or reveal the Tool bar via the menu icon in the upper right corner of the panel.

3. The Navigation pod sits beneath the Tool bar on the left edge of the panel and houses the Favorites menu. You can also hide or reveal the Navigation pod via the menu icon in the upper right corner of the panel.

4. The remainder of the panel displays thumbnails. To resize the panel and thumbnails, position the cursor over the top edge and when the cursor changes to a double-ended arrow, drag up or down.

5. Click the menu at the top of the Navigation pod to reveal the Favorites menu. To browse folders, select Computer or your login name from the menu. The bottom part of the pod will show folders. Double-click a folder in the pod to drill down into the folder and click the ellipsis (...) at the top of the panel to move up to the parent folder. You can also navigate up the folder hierarchy by clicking in the Path bar.

6 Click on a thumbnail and hit the space bar to view an image full-screen.

7 Control-click | Right-click on an image to display a contextual menu with options that include Open with Camera Raw, Add to Favorites, Photomerge and Merge to HDR Pro.

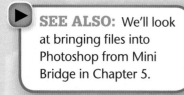
SEE ALSO: We'll look at bringing files into Photoshop from Mini Bridge in Chapter 5.

HOT TIP: The Filter menu in Mini Bridge is useful, but Mini Bridge can't recreate a Filter panel selection from Bridge. To get around this, you can make a collection of your Filter panel results before using the Boomerang button to switch back to Photoshop and then activate the collection in Mini Bridge.

3 Pre-edit in Camera Raw

Introduction

Adobe Camera Raw is a plug-in that extends the functionality of both Photoshop and Bridge. It translates the raw data captured from a camera's image sensor into a digital image that Photoshop can edit. We call this developing the image, and if you are familiar with Lightroom, Camera Raw is the functional equivalent of Lightroom's Develop module. In fact, Adobe went out of its way to make sure that all of the tools in each product match up.

Camera Raw is very powerful, and is even sufficient to make great images without opening them in Photoshop proper, but a good way to think of it is as a pre-processor that can do a lot of the initial leg work in making an image look great before you open it in Photoshop, saving you a lot of work.

The advantages of shooting in Raw over shooting in JPEG are increased dynamic range and the flexibility to re-make critical technical decisions, such as white balance, after the fact. While Camera Raw was initially designed specifically for raw data, its interface and non-destructive editing system make it a good tool for pre-processing JPEG and TIFF files, as well.

Use the slider and preview controls

Adobe has upgraded the Camera Raw engine for Creative Suite 6. Part of that upgrade is the new 2012 process version, which is better than ever at handling shadows and highlights. Its slider controls have been simplified and you can make more aggressive adjustments without some of the side effects seen with earlier versions. If you've edited your raw files with earlier versions of Camera Raw, the older process and interface will be used until you upgrade to the current (2012) process. You do that with a simple click. In the illustration, the tone and presence controls for the new process appear on the right and the older controls appear on the left.

All the slider controls in Camera Raw (and Photoshop in general) have numerous ways of operating them beyond dragging the slider itself. Knowing the techniques listed in steps 2–5 below can save you a lot of mousing around. Toggling the preview on and off as you work is a good way to evaluate whether your adjustments are improving the image.

1. If your raw files have been edited with an older version of Camera Raw, an exclamation mark icon will appear in the lower right corner of the image area. Click the icon to upgrade to the current process version. (You may be prompted to update all images to the current version, but it's best to update them one at a time.)

2. Click in a value field and use the up or down arrow keys to adjust the value in small increments. Use Shift + arrow key to adjust in larger increments.

3. Click on the label of a slider to select its input field. Type a new value.

4. Hold the mouse button down on a label and drag right or left to use the 'scrubby slider' to change the value of the field.

5. Click on the slider bar and the thumb will snap to where you clicked.

6. Double-click on a slider to snap it back to its default position.

7 After you use the scrubby slider or click on the slider bar, the field will still be selected. You can use the up or down arrow keys to make further adjustments.

8 Tap the P key to toggle the tick on the Preview box.

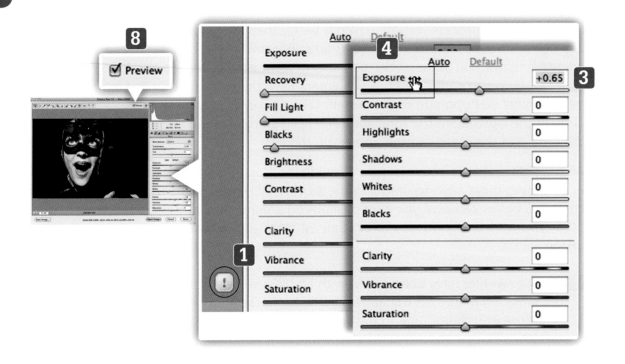

Use adjustment tabs

Most of the work of Camera Raw is done with sliding controls that are grouped into ten tabbed panels. Hover the mouse pointer over a tab to see its name in a tool tip. The tabs are described from left to right below.

1 Basic: includes white balance, exposure, vibrance.

2 Tone curves: parametric and point curves can be used together.

3 Detail: noise reduction and sharpening.

4 HSL/Grayscale: colour adjustments and Black & White conversion.

5 Split toning.

6 Lens corrections.

7 Effects: grain and post-crop vignetting.

8 Camera calibration: includes process and camera profiles.

9 Presets: you can save selected settings and apply them to other images.

10 Snapshots: save variations of your settings as you work. These apply to the current image only.

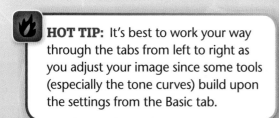

HOT TIP: It's best to work your way through the tabs from left to right as you adjust your image since some tools (especially the tone curves) build upon the settings from the Basic tab.

Adjust white balance and tint

The White Balance and Tint controls in the Basic tab work together to neutralise two aspects of light that produce colour casts in a photo. They shift the colours in the image so that the areas that are supposed to be neutral grey come out that way, and the rest of the colours fall in line. Here are some approaches to using White Balance:

1 Try different pre-sets in the White Balance menu. Each pre-set changes the shape of the histogram and assigns different settings to the Temperature and Tint sliders.

2 Click on the White Balance tool in the upper left portion of the Camera Raw interface, then click on a grey target or click on an area in your image that should be neutral grey. The new white balance will be set.

3 If you don't like the result, try clicking somewhere else. Clicking on things that are warm-toned in real life will impart a cool tone to the image, and clicking on things that are cool-toned in real life will impart a warm tone to the image.

4 Once you establish a neutral white balance for your image, you can then intentionally warm it or cool it by shifting the white balance – e.g. you could set each image to 200K above its neutral white point.

Adjust exposure and tonality

This set of controls in the Basic tab allows you to adjust the lightness, darkness and distribution of tones in your image. Typically, it is best to work from top to bottom with these controls, though you may amend earlier settings as you make subsequent adjustments. (For example, you may revise your Shadows or Exposure setting after adjusting Blacks.)

The histogram displays the distribution of tones. Notice how it changes shape as you move the sliders. When the highlights appear blown-out (pure white) or the shadows appear blocked-up (solid black), detail has been lost and this is known as clipping. Raw files have significantly more latitude compared with JPEG or TIFF files, often allowing you to recover detail. You can turn on warnings to show areas where detail has been lost.

If you're not sure which controls to move, you can click Auto to get an idea. From there, you can keep those settings, adjust individual sliders further, or click Default to start over from scratch. Double-clicking the sliders causes them to snap to their default position, and you can hold down the Shift key and double-click a slider to select the auto setting for an individual slider.

1 Tap O or click the triangle at the top right corner of the histogram to show a red overlay on clipped highlight areas.

2 Tap U or click the triangle at the top left corner of the histogram to show a blue overlay on clipped shadows.

3 Exposure: this slider affects most of the tones. The increments are in stops and simulate what happens when you alter the exposure settings in your camera.

4 Contrast: this slider covers a range that overlaps the Shadows and Highlights. As you increase contrast, shadows are darkened, while highlights are lightened. The control is focused around middle tones and does not affect deep shadows or brighter tones very much.

? DID YOU KNOW?

Clipping isn't always a bad thing. Sometimes the drama of a photo lies in the fact that part of it is plunged into complete blackness, or there is a bright spot of pure white light in the midst of it. Let the indicators advise you, but not control you.

5 Highlights: affects middle tones above 50% grey. The whites are not affected.

6 Shadows: affects middle tones below 50% grey. The blacks are not affected.

7 Whites: affects the brightest tones in the image.

8 Blacks: affects the darkest tones in the image.

9 Tap the P key to toggle the preview on and off and see a complete before/after comparison of your adjustments.

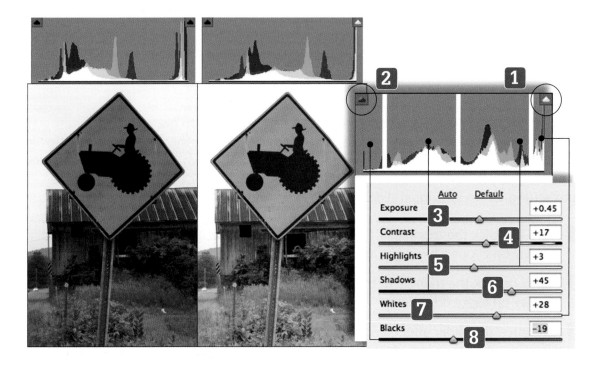

Adjust clarity, vibrance and saturation

These three Basic tab controls have to do with the richness or purity of the colours in your image. Clarity also increases contrast in a targeted way. Increasing the setting can bring out texture in a compelling way, while decreasing it can smooth out skin or other rough surface details. Vibrance increases saturation but protects skin tones and affects colours more gradually as their saturation increases. For most purposes, Vibrance is a better choice than Saturation when you want to increase the purity of the colours, though you'll sometimes add a small amount of Saturation after applying a Vibrance adjustment.

1 To adjust Clarity, zoom in to 100% or more, so you can see fine details, then move the slider to the right to increase its effect or to the left to decrease.

2 Move the Vibrance slider to the right to increase or to the left to decrease saturation. Notice how skin tones and saturated colours respond and that hints of colour remain in the image when you move the slider all the way to the left.

3 Move the Saturation slider to increase or decrease saturation. Notice how the colours change, and that it is easy to produce unpleasant, over-saturated skin colours. Pushing the Saturation slider all the way to the left produces a black and white image.

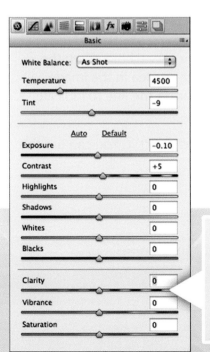

SEE ALSO: Even though you can convert an image to black and white by pulling the saturation slider all the way to the left, there are much better ways to do it. See the section on converting to grayscale later in this chapter.

HOT TIP: If you're familiar with older versions of Camera Raw, the Clarity slider used to create some unsightly haloes; the new version no longer does this.

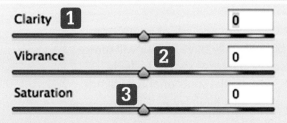

Use Tone Curves

The controls in the Tone Curves tab build upon the settings established by the tone sliders in the Basic tab. You should make your basic adjustments first, then use the tone curves to further refine your image. The parametric controls allow you to shape your curve around three movable points of inflection, while the point curve is a more free-form tool that resembles the Curves adjustment in Photoshop.

In either curve, contrast increases as the curve goes more vertical and decreases as the curve goes more horizontal. A roller coaster-shaped curve will produce solarisation effects that are often problematic but can be used creatively.

1 To activate the **parametric controls**, click the Parametric tab.

2 Drag the region dividers at the bottom of the graph area to change how the curve defines highlights, lights, darks and shadows.

3 Move the control sliders left to darken and right to lighten. Notice which part of the curve is affected by the change. You can also tap T to activate the Targeted Adjustment tool and then drag the pointer in the image to automatically select a slider and adjust it.

4 To activate the **point controls**, click the Point tab.

5 Optional: try the Medium Contrast and Strong Contrast settings with the Curve menu as a starting point for your curve. You can modify the curve manually from there.

6 To determine where you want to modify the shape of the curve, hold down the Command | Ctrl key and position the mouse pointer over an area in the image where you want to change the tone. A bubble will appear on the line to indicate which tone you are pointing at.

7 Click the mouse to place a control point on the curve and select it. You can use the up or down arrow keys to adjust the point.

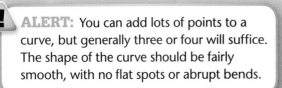

ALERT: You can add lots of points to a curve, but generally three or four will suffice. The shape of the curve should be fairly smooth, with no flat spots or abrupt bends.

8 Click on a point to select it and drag it up to lighten or down to darken.

9 If the new control point is very close to another, you may find your curve starting to kink. You'll need to delete a point to resolve the problem.

10 To delete any selected point on a curve, hit the Delete | Backspace key.

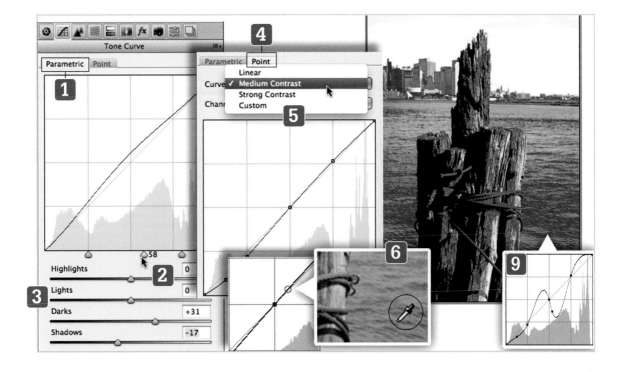

HOT TIP: Images often benefit from increased contrast. Try lightening the lights and darkening the shadows or darks. Keep an eye on your histogram and be careful not to blow out the highlights. Toggle the clipping warnings on and off for additional feedback.

Convert to greyscale (black and white)

The HSL/Grayscale tab is straightforward and produces results that are far superior to simply dragging the Saturation slider to zero in the Basic tab. It works by translating the primary and secondary hues in your image into different shades of grey, which you can individually lighten or darken. The Grayscale conversion also works with the Targeted Adjustment Tool.

1 Click on the HSL/Grayscale icon.

2 Click to tick the box labelled Convert to Grayscale.

3 Try each slider and adjust as required. Depending on the colours in your original image, some sliders will have no effect at all. Slide to the left to darken or to the right to lighten.

4 Or click the Targeted Adjustment Tool button (tap T) to activate it.

5 Drag up/down or left/right in the image to target a colour and alter its corresponding slider. (Sometimes, more than one slider will move.)

6 Toggle the Preview (tap P) to see how the conversion is working and which colours to lighten or darken.

ALERT: Make sure you toggle the Preview (tap P). If you toggle the Convert to Grayscale box instead, you will lose your adjustments.

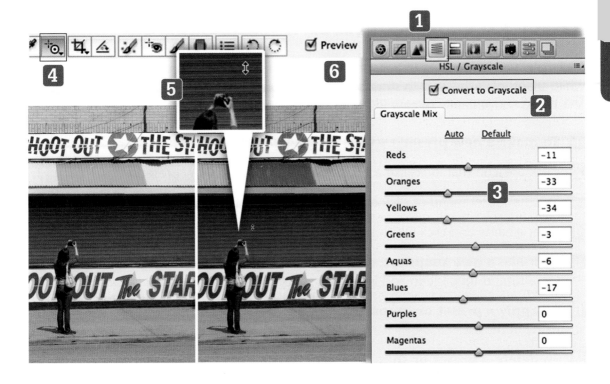

Use presets and snapshots

Presets let you name a set of adjustments and store them for reuse with other images, while snapshots allow you to store several variations of settings within a single image. Snapshots conveniently remain in the image until you delete them.

1 **To make a new preset**, click the Presets tab.

2 Click the icon that looks like a turned-up page to add a new preset.

3 Use the subset menu or click on tick boxes to tick off the adjustments you want.

4 Enter a name and click OK to save.

5 **To make a new snapshot**, click the Snapshots tab and click the icon that looks like a turned-up page to add a new snapshot. Enter a name and click OK to save.

6 **To apply a preset or snapshot**, click the corresponding tab and then click on its name in the list.

7 **To delete a preset or snapshot**, click the corresponding tab and then click on the preset or snapshot. Click the trashcan icon.

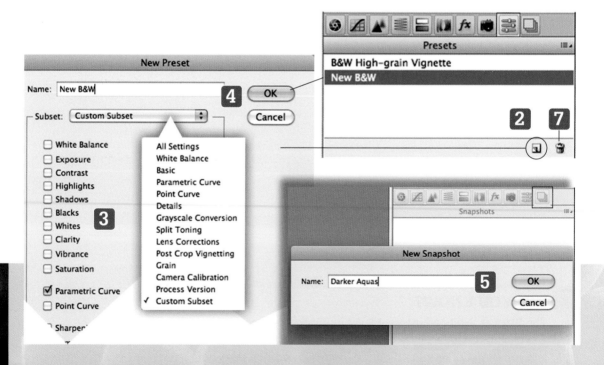

Synchronise white balance, etc.

You can select multiple images in Bridge and open them in Camera Raw. The images appear in a vertical strip on the left side on the dialogue. You can then edit images individually or select several and adjust them as a group, and you can synchronise settings between multiple files. Once you have synchronised settings, you can click on individual images to adjust them further.

1 Select multiple images in Bridge by selecting one and then using Shift-click or Command | Control-click to select the rest.

2 Click the Open in Camera Raw icon or use Command | Ctrl + R.

3 To begin synchronising settings, click on your reference image (e.g. one containing a white balance target) and adjust settings such as white balance, exposure, grayscale conversion, etc.

4 To select all or some of the other images in the group, click Select All (Command | Ctrl + A) or use Shift-click or Command | Control-click to select. Your reference image will have a blue outline around it.

5 Optional: if you want to change the reference image without starting the selection process again, Option | Alt-click on a thumbnail to designate it as the new reference.

6 Click Synchronise.

7 Use the Synchronise menu or tick off the boxes to select the settings you want to synchronise.

8 Click OK to complete the synchronisation process.

9 Click Done to exit Camera Raw and update the XMP data for all the images.

Reset, cancel or save settings without opening Photoshop

In some workflows (e.g. when making a quick web gallery or PDF) you may need to make adjustments in Camera Raw for the moment and put the images aside for later. In other cases, you need to start again from scratch with your settings, or exit Camera Raw without updating the settings.

1 To save your adjustments without opening Photoshop, click the Done button or hit the Return | Enter key.

2 To discard your adjustments, click the Cancel button or hit the Esc key.

3 To reset the dialogue, hold down the Option | Alt key – the Cancel button will become a Reset button – and click the Reset button.

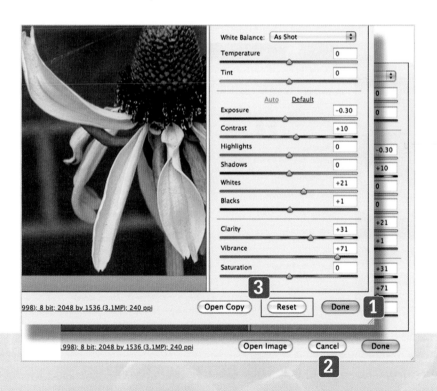

Use the Save Image button

In some cases, Camera Raw's editing features are sufficient to do all the creative work you need without passing the file on to Photoshop. The Save Image feature allows you to create JPEG, TIFF, DNG and Photoshop files directly from the Camera Raw environment.

1 Click Save Image. The Save Options dialogue will appear.

2 In the Destination section, you can click Select Folder to designate a location or select Save in Same Location from the menu.

3 Set your file-naming policy as required. Enter text into the boxes or select values from the menus. As you fill in the boxes, the example will update.

4 Use the Format section to specify what kind of file you want to save and set any related options. Notice that you can strip location data.

5 Click Save. A progress indicator will appear next to the Save Image button.

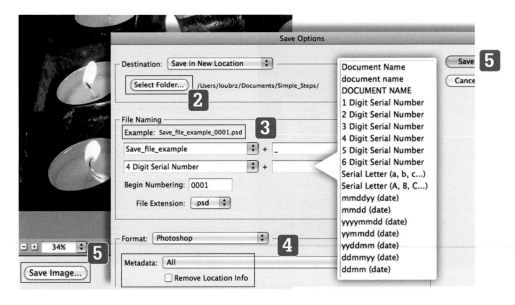

 HOT TIP: When you open and select multiple images in Camera Raw, the Save Image button will process all the files in one shot.

 DID YOU KNOW?

Camera Raw will remember the Save Options you selected. If you want to bypass the Save Options dialogue and use the same settings, hold down the Option | Alt key as you click the Save Image button.

4 Manage colours in Photoshop

Introduction

If you've ever walked into a store or even a pub with lots of TV sets on display, you've seen why colour management is necessary: the same image can look dramatically different, depending on how each set translates colour information. Another example is trying to get prints to match what you see on your screen. When it comes to colour, each output device effectively speaks a different dialect, and without colour management each will interpret colour information differently.

At its heart, digital colour is an adaptation of the old paint-by-numbers technique. A digital photo is a mosaic consisting of millions of pixels, each tagged with an RGB number that represents its colour. RGB numbers are used because they are efficient, but they only represent colours indirectly by specifying how much red, green and blue to mix. The problem with this formula-based approach to colour is that no two devices will render a set of RGB numbers in the same way, and the variatons can be great.

There is another way to represent colour, and it is the key to colour management. Devices known as colorimeters and spectrophotometers can measure colours and represent them in terms of a precise 3D coordinate system known as Lab values or Lab coordinates. In essence, Lab values describe colours in numerical terms and they are based on the way human beings see, not on how colours are mixed. That makes them the perfect reference for colour management.

Entire books have been written on colour management, so we obviously can't treat the subject in depth, but in this chapter we'll look briefly at some practical fundamentals.

Understand colour management

Colour management systems keep colours accurate and consistent between different devices such as screens, printers, etc. by translating the RGB numbers in an image to the correct RGB numbers for each device. Computer screens, printers, projectors and other devices each have a colour gamut – a distinct range of colours that they can reproduce. Software tools can analyse the colour numbers within a gamut to produce colour profiles, which work much like the keys that define symbols on a map – they correlate colour numbers with Lab coordinates. As you edit images in Photoshop, you'll probably use one of two working spaces – Adobe RGB or ProPhoto RGB. These are special reference colour profiles that define a range of usable colours rather than describing the colour characteristics of a specific device. You'll usually embed one of these into your master files when you save them.

To present colours accurately on your screen, a colour management system can first use the embedded colour profile in an image (the source) to translate its colour numbers into Lab coordinates. It can then use your screen's colour profile (the destination) to look up the RGB numbers that correspond to the Lab coordinates from your image. If the destination space does not contain a particular Lab value, the colour is said to be out of gamut, and a strategy called the Rendering Intent is used to substitute an available colour.

When you save copies of your images for the web, colour management can convert the colour numbers in the web image to conform to the sRGB colour space. Similarly, when you print, colour management will convert the colour numbers in your image to the corresponding colour numbers for the printer profile that you select.

Colour management is built into Photoshop, Windows and Mac OS. Some web browsers use it and some don't. As the time of writing, iOS (e.g. iPhone and iPad) and Android devices do not. The colour strategies presented below are designed to take advantage of colour management when it is available and to minimise colour issues when it's not.

- The single most effective way to get better colour results is to calibrate and profile your computer monitor. You'll want to use a device to profile your display and stay away from software-only solutions.

- When editing images, Adobe RGB is the best general-purpose 'working space'. ProPhoto RGB is able to retain the widest gamut of colours, but it requires you to work in 16-bit mode at all times. Both of these colour spaces were designed to allow you to print colours that your camera has captured, even if your display cannot show them.

- You should always embed the colour space you used to edit your image when you save your master documents.

- For printers, each combination of paper and ink constitutes a distinct set of colour characteristics, so you'll want an accurate profile for each type of paper you use with your printer. Many, but not all, of the colour profiles provided by paper manufacturers are quite good. If you're interested in high-quality profiles, there are tools that can build profiles for both your display and your printer.

- Any time you convert the colours in an image, there is a chance of colours shifting or being lost. For that reason, you should convert colours as few times as possible and never save over your master file after you convert to a different colour space.

- Assume that your files are not likely to be properly colour managed when you share them via the Web or as email attachments. Software that does not do colour management will typically assume that all image files are in sRGB. For this reason, it's best to convert files to sRGB when you're saving them for sharing. Files in Adobe RGB or other colour spaces look wrong when viewed in software that does not colour manage.

? DID YOU KNOW?

One of the best-known formats for colour profiles is ICC profiles, a standard developed by the International Color Consortium. ICC profiles are widely used, but there are other colour profile formats, such as Adobe's DNG profiles for cameras.

Calibrate and profile your display

Calibrating and profiling your display is one of the simplest things to do, and it makes a tremendous difference, because it maximises the accuracy of the colours you're seeing as you adjust images. This is true whether you're using a consumer-grade computer monitor with an sRGB colour gamut or a professional display that can reproduce nearly all the colours in Adobe RGB. It's worth investing in a hardware tool to calibrate and profile your monitor. Systems such as x-Rite's ColorMunki display and i1Display Pro are fast, accurate and take the guesswork out of the process. The X-Rite ColorMunki Photo is more advanced and can make profiles for displays, printers and even digital projectors.

A common complaint is that prints come out looking dark compared with the screen. That's because computer screens generally come from the manufacturer with the brightness set way too high. For many flat-screen displays, the only setting you can control (and thus calibrate) is the brightness. Setting the target luminance in your profiling software to somewhere between 100 and 120 lumens will make a tremendous difference. You should also operate your screen in somewhat dimmed room light that does not overpower your screen. No direct light should hit the display – you shouldn't see reflections in its surface. Some screens have an ambient light sensor that tries to automatically adjust the brightness of your screen – you should turn off this feature.

We'll walk through a typical profiling process using the ColorMunki Photo. Depending upon the tool you use, there will be some differences in the process, but the principles will be the same:

1 Launch the ColorMunki software.

2 Click Profile My Display.

3 Select the display you want to profile and click Next.

HOT TIP: Displays' colour performance can change over time, so it's also a good idea to re-profile your monitor from time to time.

4 Set the following preferences, then click Next:

- Display profiling mode: Advanced.
- Target luminance level: 100. (You can select a higher level if matching prints is not important.)
- Target white point for display: Native (for wider gamut) or D65 (industry standard).

5 Calibrate the device and click Next.

6 Position the device on the screen and click Next.

7 Adjust the brightness when prompted and click Next.

8 Click Save when prompted.

9 Set the Remind me option as you like and click Next.

10 Review Before and After, then click Next to finish.

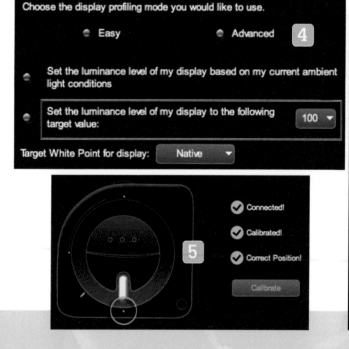

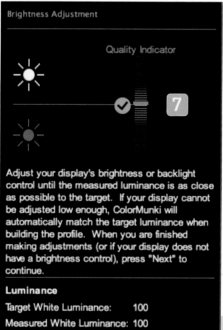

> **! ALERT:** Software-only display 'calibration' tools that rely on your eyes, such as Windows Display Colour Calibration, Adobe Gamma and Apple's Calibration assistant, are unreliable at best and can actually make things worse.

Convert colours for sharing

It's important to convert your images to the sRGB colour space when you save them for sharing because many web browsers and email applications assume your images are in sRGB instead of colour managing. Images in Adobe RGB will simply not look right when displayed by those applications. It's still a good idea to embed the sRGB colour profile, so that software that does understand colour management can still use it.

1 The dialogue for the File, Save for Web command includes a simple option you can tick to convert to sRGB.

2 For full control over your colour conversion process, you can use Photoshop's Edit, Convert to Profile command before using the File, Save As command. In the next section, we'll look at how you can use soft proofing to preview and adjust your results before executing the Convert to Profile command.

3 Bridge has a Save to Hard Disk module in its Export panel. The module automatically converts files to sRGB.

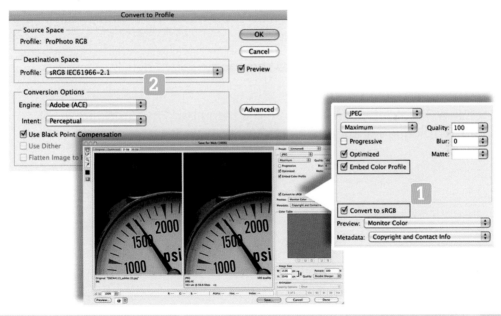

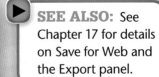

ALERT: If you use the Convert to Profile command on your master file, you should never overwrite it by using File, Save. Not only can you lose colour fidelity, but Photoshop often discards your layers to preserve appearance. Either use the History panel to revert the file to its original colour profile or use File | Save As to save the converted file as a new document.

SEE ALSO: See Chapter 17 for details on Save for Web and the Export panel.

Use soft proofing to manage colour conversion

When you convert from a large colour space to a smaller one, there is always the potential for colour shifts. This can happen in the case of preparing sRGB photos for the Web, or even when you make a print. A large part of this comes from certain colours not being available in the smaller space. When that happens, similar colours that are available in the smaller space are substituted. Soft proofing simulates the conversion on your screen to help you pre-visualise the result. Rather than simply accept the way Photoshop has converted the colours, you can add adjustment layers to your soft proof to steer the colour conversion. Your final result may not be a perfect match, but you can often produce a better translation than the default.

1. Select Image, Duplicate from the menu bar. A dialogue will appear. You have the option to enter a name that makes sense into the box. Click OK to finish duplicating the image. This will be your proof copy.

2. Select Window, Arrange, 2-up Vertical from the menu bar to display the images side by side with the proof copy on the left.

3. Zoom and position the proof copy to show some salient details, then select Window, Arrange, Match All.

4. Select View, Proof Setup, Custom from the menu bar. The Customize Proof Condition dialogue will appear.

WHAT DOES THIS MEAN?

Out of gamut: colour spaces define a gaumut, or range of colours, numerically. When you convert the colours in an image from one colour space to another, there are likely to be colours in the starting colour space (e.g. ProPhoto RGB) that are not available in the destination colour space (e.g. your printer's colour profile). Any colours that are not included within a colour space are said to be out of gamut. When you turn on the Gamut Warning feature in Photoshop, it will indicate the parts of the image that contain colours that fall outside the gamut of the destination colour space.

5. In the Proof Conditions dialogue, do the following:
   - Select a colour profile from the Device to Simulate menu. This can be a target colour space like sRGB or a device profile such as a printer and paper combination.
   - Choose a Rendering Intent. There are only two that concern photographers: Perceptual handles gradients best, but can cause more pronounced colour shifts; Relative Colorimetric shifts colours less, but can cause gradients to turn into flat bands of colour, a condition known as banding or posterisation.
   - Avoid ticking the Preserve RGB Numbers, Simulate Paper Color and Simulate Black Ink options.
   - Click OK to activate the soft proof.

6. Add adjustment layers to correct for any outstanding issues. One common problem is that some blues can skew towards purple. You can add a Hue/Saturation layer to target the colour and change its hue to one that works better.

7. If some of your adjustments seem unresponsive in certain areas, it may be because they are out of gamut. You can select View, Gamut Warning to toggle an overlay that shows out-of-gamut regions in grey.

8. When you are satisfied with the soft proof, choose Edit, Convert to Profile from the menu bar. The dialogue that appears should contain the same settings as the Customize Proof Condition dialogue. Confirm your settings and click OK to complete the conversion.

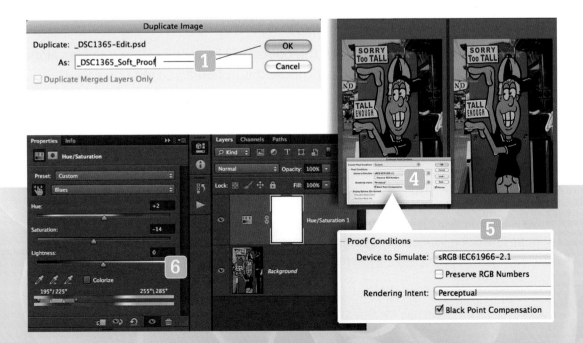

Dealing with missing colour profiles

It's not unusual to find files that have been prepared for the Web and are untagged. This will happen if you untick the box to embed the colour profile as you save an image. Such files may or may not display the correct colours, even with colour management turned on. To resolve the issue, you can assign a colour profile. It is a non-destructive process, since you're simply changing the associations between colour numbers in the image and Lab coordinates in the profile. However, you want to be sure you assign the right profile before converting the colours to a different one.

When you open an untagged image with Photoshop, you have the option to assign a colour profile immediately, or to wait and evaluate the image to determine which colour profile looks best.

1 Select Edit, Color Settings to review Photoshop's colour management settings and policies.

- Notice your working space. If you are following the recommendation from earlier in this book, it will be Adobe RGB.

- Adjust your preferences. If Ask When Opening next to Missing Profiles is ticked, Photoshop will present a dialogue whenever it encounters an untagged file.

- Click OK to close the dialogue.

2 With the Ask When Opening preference above, you'll see the Missing Profile dialogue if you open an untagged image:

- Leave as is (don't color manage): this option will leave the colour numbers alone and simply open the file. You can choose this option if you're not sure and evaluate the image in Photoshop.

- Assign working RGB: this option assigns the working space that you set up in the Color Settings dialogue.

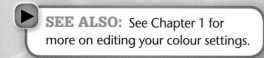

SEE ALSO: See Chapter 1 for more on editing your colour settings.

- Assign profile: you can select any colour profile installed on your machine from the menu.

3 Once the file is open, you can choose Edit, Assign Profile from the menu bar to add a profile to an untagged image or change the currently assigned profile. The dialogue has the same three options as the Missing Profile dialogue, along with a Preview option that you can tick on and off.

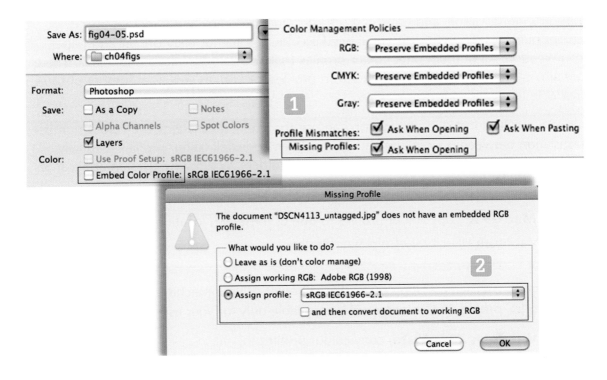

Install colour profiles

Accurate profiles ensure that you get the best possible colour performance out of your printer. When you install your printer software, colour profiles for the manufacturer's own papers are typically installed for you. One of the most likely situations where you may install a colour profile is when you want to use paper made by another company. A number of high-quality papers come from manufacturers such as Hahnemühle Fine Art, Ilford, Crane, and Canson. Each combination of ink and paper interprets colour numbers differently, so you'll need a colour profile for each printer and paper combination. All of them offer colour profiles that you can download and install. There are also companies that can make custom profiles for you, as well as a number of tools available to create your own profiles.

Once a profile is installed, Photoshop can use the profile to manage the colour number translation between your image and your printer. To install colour profiles manually, you simply copy the file to one of the specified folders. Windows 7 uses an application to install them.

1. On **Mac OS X**, copy colour profiles to one of these two locations:
   - Macintosh HD/Library/ColorSync/Profiles
     or
   - <your username>/Library/ColorSync/Profiles (If your machine has more than one login, profiles in this folder will be available only for your user name/login.)

2. On **Windows** XP or **Vista**, copy colour profiles to:
   - \Windows\system32\spool\drivers\color

3. In **Windows 7**, use the Colour Management control panel:
   - From the Start menu, select Control Panel and click on Color Management.
   - Click the All Profiles tab, then click Add.
   - Use the dialogue to locate the profile. Select it and click Add.
   - Click Close.

5 Bring images into Photoshop

Introduction

Even though Photoshop has a File, Open command, it's actually rare that you'll open images that way. This chapter is about the broad range of other methods for bringing images in. Beyond simply opening the files, Photoshop can process them in a range of ways:

- process raw files and transfer them into Photoshop
- place files as smart objects
- bring multiple images into a single Photoshop document
- create panoramas, diptychs, collages, etc.

Open images from Bridge, Mini Bridge, Finder and Windows

1 Double-click a file in Mini Bridge or the Content panel in Bridge to open it in Photoshop. If the file is a raw file, it will open in Camera Raw. JPEG and TIFF files that have been previously edited in Camera Raw will also open in Camera Raw.

2 Control-click | Right-click an image in Mini Bridge to display a menu and select Open With, Photoshop.

3 Control-click | Right-click a file in the Mac Finder or Windows Explorer to reveal a menu that includes an option to open the file with Photoshop.

4 On a Mac, you can drag a file to the Photoshop icon in the Dock to instruct Photoshop to open it.

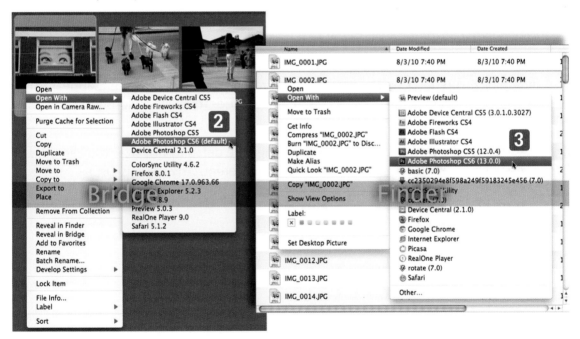

 HOT TIP: To open JPEG and TIFF files into Camera Raw instead of Photoshop, Control-click | Right-click a thumbnail to display a menu in Mini Bridge or the Content panel of Bridge:

- Select Open in Camera Raw from the menu in Bridge.
- Select Open With, Camera Raw from the menu in Mini Bridge.

Set workflow options and open images from Camera Raw

In the previous section, we saw that raw files always open in Camera Raw because it converts their data into an image format that Photoshop understands. You may also want to edit JPEG or TIFF files in Camera Raw because of its interface and non-destructive editing capabilities. Once you finish working in Camera Raw, you can get Camera Raw to create a new file and hand it off to Photoshop. You'll use the workflow options to determine the colour space and bit depth of that file.

1 Click the underlined text at the bottom of the Camera Raw dialogue to reveal the Workflow Options dialogue.

2 Select a colour space and bit depth for the new document. Adobe RGB and 16 bits per channel are recommended for general purposes. (ProPhoto RGB supports even more colours, but can be used only in 16-bit mode, whereas Adobe RGB can be used in either 16-bit or 8-bit mode.)

3 Leave the size set to its default. You should not see a + or − sign to the right of the dimensions. You don't want Camera Raw to resample it. (The sizes that appear in the menu depend on the original size of your image. Your dimensions will probably be different.)

4 Leave the resolution as-is. It merely determines the default print size. You can adjust that when you print. (Your resolution may be different. Any value is OK.)

5 The Sharpen For menu should be set to none. You'll sharpen in Photoshop at the end of your editing/adjustment process.

6 Leave Open in Photoshop as Smart Objects unticked.

7 Click OK to accept the Workflow Settings.

 HOT TIP: The sharpening and resampling options in the Workflow Options dialogue were designed for use with the Save Image button. You won't use them with the Open Image button.

8 To open your image in Photoshop:

- Click Open Image to save your settings and open the image in Photoshop.
- Hold down the Option | Alt key to convert the button to Open Copy. Click the button to open the image in Photoshop without saving the settings.
- Hold down the Shift key to convert the button to Open Object. Click the button to embed a Camera Raw smart object into your Photoshop document.

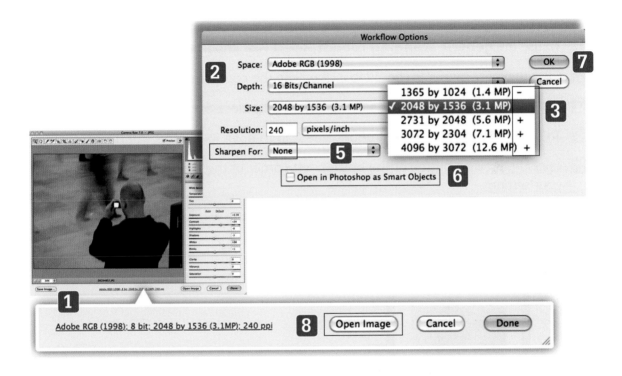

SEE ALSO: The Smart Objects option embeds a Camera Raw object into your Photoshop document. When you double-click the smart object, it will reopen in Camera Raw. See Chapter 7 for more info on smart objects.

Import images from scanners

Another way of getting files into Photoshop is to scan them directly with the File, Import command. When you need to scan a single image and bring it into Photoshop, it can be tedious to run standalone scanner software, save a scan file and then open it in Photoshop. A built-in software toolkit called ImageKit provides basic scanning functionality. If you install VueScan, Photoshop will find it and automatically add a menu item for it.

1 To use the **generic scanning toolkit**, select File, Import Images from Device.

2 Click on your scanner in the sidebar, then use the controls to adjust.

3 Click scan to import the image and automatically close the dialogue

4 To use **VueScan**, select File, Import, VueScan to open its scanner interface.

5 Click the Preview button at the bottom left corner of the window and then adjust your settings.

6 Click the Scan button at the bottom left corner of the window to capture the scan.

7 Hit Esc or close the dialogue to exit VueScan and transfer the image into Photoshop.

Place files

You can combine multiple images into one Photoshop file by placing them. Photoshop's default behaviour is to convert the images to smart objects as you do so. That allows you to transform them and apply filters repeatedly without the kind of degradation you would see with ordinary layers. You can start by opening an existing file by choosing File, New to create an empty file.

1 To begin placing a file, do any of the following:

- Drag files to Photoshop's canvas from Mini Bridge, Bridge, the Finder or Windows Explorer. You can drag multiple files together.
- Control-click | Right-click in the Content panel of Bridge or the thumbnail area of Mini Bridge to display a menu and select Place, In Photoshop.

2 The file will appear on the canvas in Free Transform mode. Do any of the following:

- Drag the file into position
- Hold down the Shift key and drag any corner handle to scale the image.
- Control-click | Right-click on the object to change the transformation mode.

3 Hit Return | Enter to finish placing the object. The control handles will disappear. Or tap the Esc key to cancel.

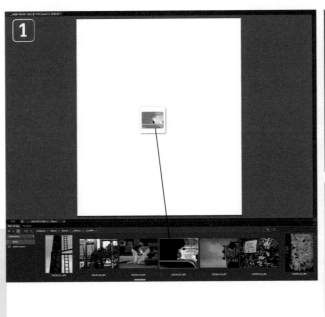

Load files into Photoshop layers

You can make a selection of thumbnails in either Mini Bridge or Bridge and then open those files together into a single Photoshop file with one command. The files will load as layers stacked directly above each other, with the layers named after the files they came from.

Once you load the layers together, you can convert the layers to smart objects as needed, reorder and scale them to create collages, or change the canvas size to create diptychs, triptychs, etc. You can also overlap the layers and add masking to merge them in various ways. To load a selection of files as layers:

1 Select several images in Mini Bridge or Bridge. (Click one and then either Command-click | Control-click or Shift-click to select additional images.)

2 In Mini Bridge, Control-click | Right-click on one of the selected thumbnails to reveal a contextual menu and select Photoshop, Load Files into Photoshop Layers.

3 In Bridge, Select Tools, Photoshop, Load Files into Photoshop Layers from menu bar.

Generate collages and panoramas

Photoshop can do a lot of the work of melding images into panoramas and collages for you. The Photomerge command can automatically match and mask a selected group of images into a cohesive arrangement. From there, you have the option to straighten and enhance the image even further.

1 Select two or more images in either Mini Bridge or Bridge.

2 Open the Photomerge dialogue:
- In Mini Bridge, Control-click | Right-click on one of the selected thumbnails and select Photoshop, Photomerge from the menu.
- In Bridge, select Tools, Photoshop, Photomerge from the menu bar.

3 Use the dialogue box to add or remove files from the list and set processing parameters (e.g. Auto Layout + Blend Images Together).

4 Click OK to process the files.

5 Optional: activate the Crop tool and use its Straighten tool to level the horizon.

6 The resulting composite is made up of masked layers. You can revise the masks, add layers, etc. as you see fit.

 HOT TIP: For best results with panorama stitching, Photoshop needs about 40% overlap. If images overlap 70% or more, they may not blend. It's also best not to move or zoom in or out as you take the frames. Try to keep your panning level and your exposure consistent – the odd shapes of the segments in the example show what can happen when your panning isn't level. You can sometimes use Content-Aware Fill to clean up messy edges.

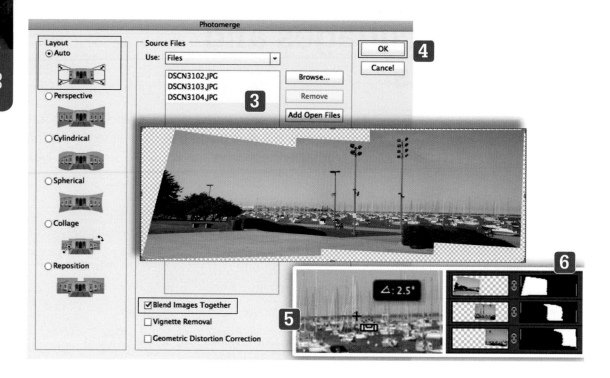

6 Crop, straighten, erase and undo

Introduction

In Chapter 3, we looked at how you can crop in Camera Raw at the beginning of the workflow. That's a good place to do it, but Camera Raw can't edit Photoshop files or layered TIFFs, and there will be times when it makes more sense to crop later in the process anyway. In CS6, Photoshop's Crop tool has some new options that distinguish it further from its Camera Raw sibling.

Despite all the emphasis on non-destructive editing and using masks to hide rather than remove pixels, there are still good reasons to erase. There are also times when editing goes awry and you discover that you've erased or deleted something that you still need. The History panel can provide a wide array of methods, beyond a simple undo, for rolling your work back.

Trim, crop or straighten an image

The Trim command will snip edges (e.g. a white border) from an image based on transparency or colour. A simple crop command will trim your image to conform to a selection, or you can use the feature-rich Crop tool to completely reshape your composition.

A lot of photographers crop as a way to remove unwanted items from an image, but that can leave an unbalanced composition. Crop tool overlays can guide you in defining more effective new compositions. The interface for the Crop tool has been substantially revised in Photoshop CS6. If you prefer the old Crop tool behaviour, tick the box marked Use Classic Mode in the dialogue under the gear menu in the Options bar.

1 Select Image, Trim from the menu bar to use it.

2 For a simple crop, make a selection and then choose Image, Crop from the menu bar. This method always discards the cropped pixels.

3 Tap C or click in the Tool panel to activate the Crop tool.

4 In the Options Bar, select Unconstrained or a fixed aspect ratio from the menu, or enter proportions into the boxes.

5 To resample as you crop, tap R or select Size & Resolution from the aspect ratio menu.

6 Tap X or use the Rotate button to switch the crop orientation between horizontal and vertical (landscape and portrait).

7 Click the gear icon to set additional interface options.

8 To hide cropped pixels, untick the box marked Delete Cropped Pixels.

 HOT TIP: If you make a selection before you activate the Crop tool, it will use the selection to define the area you want to crop. If you don't delete pixels when you crop, you use the Move tool to reposition the crop – just make sure you select and move all layers in the image. To restore hidden pixels, select Image, Reveal All.

9 Adjust the crop:

- Drag the handles to reshape the crop.
- When the aspect ratio is unconstrained, hold the Shift key and drag the corner handles to scale the crop and retain the same shape.
- Drag inwards to trim away pixels or outwards to expand the canvas.
- Once you move the crop handles, the overlay lines will appear. Tap O to cycle through the overlays or use the View menu in the Options bar. For overlays like the Diagonal and Golden Spiral, tap Shift + O to change the orientation of the overlay.
- To straighten, Hold the Command | Ctrl key and drag in the image to define what's horizontal or vertical. Photoshop will show the angle as you drag and rotate the image when you release the mouse button.
- Drag inside the crop area to reposition the crop.
- Use the arrow keys to nudge the crop one pixel at a time, or hold down the Shift key and tap the arrow keys to bump it ten pixels at a time.
- Move the mouse pointer outside the corners and drag to rotate the image as you crop.

10 Hit the Return | Enter key to apply the cropping.

Erase three ways

The simplest and most direct way to remove pixels is with the Eraser tool. It's based on the Brush tool and can be applied in a number of creative ways using brush presets. Reducing the hardness of the eraser creates a feathered edge. You can also make a selection and then delete pixels with a keystroke or use the selection like masking tape to protect parts of your image from being erased.

In many cases, you might opt to use a layer mask to hide pixels instead of permanently deleting them first. When you no longer need the flexibility afforded by the mask, you can erase the pixels by applying the mask.

1 Tap E or click the button in the Tools panel to activate the Eraser tool.

2 Use the Eraser in Brush mode and paint with brush tips for effects such as erosion. In the Options bar, you can reduce opacity and airbrush-style build-up mode with reduced flow.

3 You can zoom in and use the Eraser in Block mode to clear areas pixel by pixel.

4 Make a selection (e.g. with the Quick Selection, Lasso or Marquee tools) and hit the Delete | Backspace key to remove pixels.

5 You can also make a selection to confine where you erase. The eraser will only remove pixels inside the selected area. Don't forget to deselect (Command | Ctrl + D) afterwards.

6 To erase pixels with a mask, Control-click | Right-click on a layer mask and select Apply Layer Mask from the menu. The command also discards the mask.

> ▶ **SEE ALSO:** Chapter 7 covers layers, Chapter 9 covers brushes, Chapter 11 covers selections and Chapter 12 covers masks.

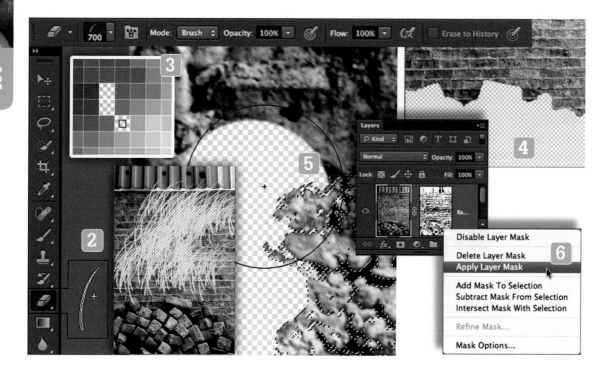

Use undo, redo and the History panel

As soon as you open a file, Photoshop opens a transcript of the changes you make to the file. Each change to your file appears as a new state at the bottom of the History panel.

When you undo a change, Photoshop reverts to the previous state, but if you immediately undo again, Photoshop performs a redo and restores the state you started from. If you want to step back to earlier states, you can use the Step Backward keystroke or click in the History panel. When you click on an earlier state in the History panel, the file reverts to that state and the subsequent states are dimmed. If you make another change to the image, the dimmed states are discarded. In Chapter 1, we looked at the History States preference that controls how many changes Photoshop will remember before it discards the oldest state to make room for the next new state. You can also record snapshots, which won't be discarded during your editing session. However, your history states and snapshots are all discarded whenever you close a file.

You can selectively undo or redo parts of the image by activating the Eraser and ticking Erase to History in the Options bar, painting with the History brush, or setting the Use menu to History when you select Edit, Fill from the menu bar.

1. Select Edit, Undo | Redo (Command | Ctrl + Z) from the menu bar.

2. Select Edit, Step Backward (Option + Command + Z | Alt + Ctrl + Z) from the menu bar.

3. Select Edit, Step Forward (Shift + Command + Z | Shift + Ctrl + Z) from the menu bar.

4. Select Photoshop, Preferences, Performance (Windows: Edit, Preferences, Performance) to change the number of history states that Photoshop retains.

5. Click on the History Panel tab or select Window, History from the menu bar to show the panel.

 HOT TIP: To set the History panel to save snapshots each time you save a file, choose History Options from the menu in the upper right corner of the History panel. That can be a very helpful tool for recovering from mistakes. If you discover that you've lost a layer and it's only in your snapshot states, you can recover it: create a new document from that state, split the screens and drag the layer back into your work file.

6. Click on the camera icon at the bottom of the panel to save a snapshot or Option | Alt-click on the icon to name the snapshot when you save it.

7. Click on the label of a history state or snapshot to revert to that state. To step backwards, click one history state at a time from bottom to top.

8. Click the box on the left edge of a history state to specify where History-based editing tools (e.g. Erase to History) will draw their data from.

9. Activate a history state and click the icon at the bottom of the panel to create a new document from that state. See the Alert box for more details.

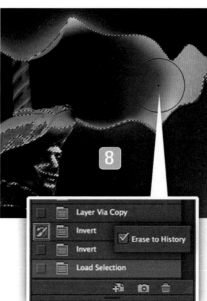

ALERT: Don't forget to save at regular intervals. If you create a new document from a history state, make sure you restore the current history state in your original document before you make any more changes.

7 Work with layers and groups

Introduction

This chapter will explore ways of working with layers, emphasising best practices and a non-destructive editing process. Working in layers and pixel-level editing are key capabilities that set Photoshop apart from programs such as Apple's Aperture and Adobe's own Photoshop Lightroom. Layers allow you to composite elements on top of your original to produce a finished result without directly altering the original. This sets the stage for being able to roll back or even store multiple variations of an image in a single file.

Photoshop can create several distinct kinds of layers: Pixel, Adjustment, Fill, Type, Shape and Video. Layers can alter the appearance of the layers beneath them in different ways. They can also be converted into smart objects, which allow you to perform actions such as applying filters or repeated scaling without degradation. Layers can be gathered into groups, and you'll see them mentioned a fair amount in this chapter.

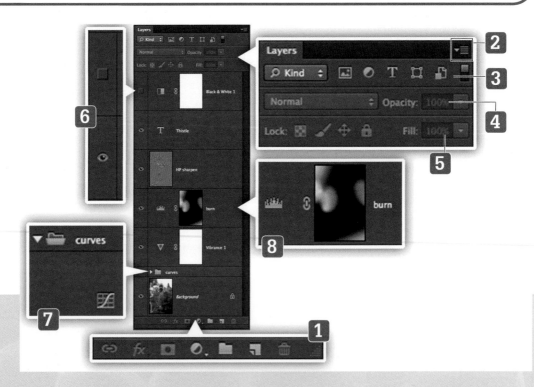

Use the layers panel

The Layers panel is the central interface for creating and managing layers. Even though there are items in the menu bar that do the same things, the emphasis in this chapter will be on using this panel. Nearly everything you want to do with layers can be done from there. Hover the mouse pointer over items in the Layers panel for a tool tip explaining what they are.

1 Using the icons at the bottom of the panel, add blank layers, groups and adjustment layers, and add masks to them. You can also duplicate, link or delete layers, as well as add layer styles.

2 Select layer-related commands from the menu icon in the upper right corner of the panel.

3 Use the controls at the top of the panel to find and filter layers.

4 Click to select a layer and then adjust the layer's blending mode or opacity with the controls in the second tier at the top of the panel.

5 Lock pixels, transparency and position of a layer via the icons just beneath the blending mode menu.

6 Click the eyeball icon to toggle visibility of layers, groups, layer styles, etc.

7 Click disclosure triangles to expand or collapse groups, layer styles, smart filters, etc.

8 Edit layer masks to control where the effects of adjustment layers are applied in the image. You can also add masks to pixel layers and groups.

9 Control-click | Right-click on thumbnails, masks and layer names to display different context-sensitive menus.

 HOT TIP: Adjustment layers and layer masks have controls that appear in the Properties panel when you select them, just as the Options bar updates when you select a button in the Tools panel.

 SEE ALSO: See Chapter 14 for more on working with text. The Type (text) and Shape (Rectangle, Ellipse, Polygon, Line, etc.) tools also create layers. Videos also appear as layers when you bring them into Photoshop.

Duplicate all or part of a layer

Many tasks in retouching begin with duplicating a layer such as the background. This is a way of creating an internal backup for your file. You can use the eyeball icon to hide the original layer and then apply destructive edits (e.g. Shadows/Highlights, filters, the Patch tool) to the copy. If you don't like the edit, you can delete the copy, re-duplicate the original and start again.

The same keystroke that duplicates an entire layer will allow you to duplicate just part of the layer – all you have to do is make a selection first. You can also cut pieces out of a layer and put them into a separate layer.

1 To duplicate an entire layer, do either of the following:

- Drag the layer to the New Layer icon at the bottom of the panel and release the mouse button when the tip of the mouse pointer touches the icon.

- Click the layer to select it, then select Layer, New, Layer via Copy (Command | Ctrl + J) from the menu bar. *Note*: If you use the New Layer via Copy command and discover that only part of the layer was copied, undo and then use the Select, Deselect command (Command | Ctrl + D) before repeating the New Layer via Copy command.

2 To copy part of a layer into a new layer, make a selection and then choose Layer, New, Layer via Copy (Command | Ctrl + J) from the menu bar.

3 To cut out part of a layer and move it to a new layer, make a selection and then select Layer, New, Layer via Cut (Shift + Command | Ctrl + J) from the menu bar.

4 Once an element is copied or cut into a new layer, you can use Free Transform (Command | Ctrl + T) to reposition and reshape it. You can also use the Eraser or a mask to clean up its edges and fit it into its new location.

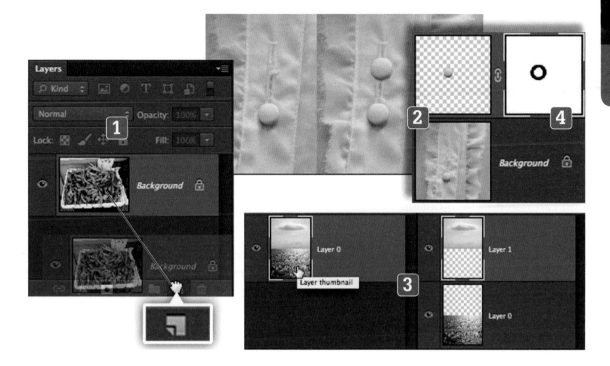

HOT TIP: Sometimes it is useful to convert the background layer into a conventional layer. Double-click on the Background to convert the layer via an options dialogue or hold down Option | Alt and double-click to bypass the dialogue.

Mix layers with opacity and blending modes

When you place two or more pixel layers together in Photoshop, the layer on top completely obscures the layer beneath, unless you reduce the opacity or change the blending mode of the top layer. Reducing the opacity makes layers more translucent, while blending modes combine the content of the layers in different ways to produce sometimes dramatic results. If the effect of a particular blending mode is too strong, you can rein it in by reducing the opacity of the top layer. Hard Mix and Vivid Light are two modes that also have a distinct response to the Fill setting.

You can use blending modes with adjustment layers and groups (covered in the next chapter), too. When you set a group to one of the blending modes other than Pass Through, the blending modes work as expected inside the group. Photoshop blends the group as if it were merged into a single layer.

The blending modes are grouped in the menu as follows:

1 Normal and Dissolve: Dissolve works only with layers that have reduced opacity or feathered areas. (The example shows a layer with a feathered mask.)

2 The darkening group (e.g. Color burn): dark areas shadow the underlying layers. White in the top layer vanishes.

3 The lightening group (e.g. Lighten): highlights in the top layers brighten the underlying layers. Black in the top layer vanishes.

4 The contrast group (e.g. Overlay): lights lighten, darks darken, 50% grey vanishes.

5 The comparative group (e.g. Difference): these abstract blending modes compare the pixels in the active layer to those below, transforming colour and tone. The Difference mode paints matching pixels black. Exclusion works similarly, but greys and inverts colours. Subtract darkens and Divide lightens.

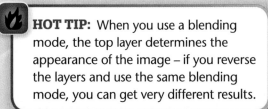

HOT TIP: When you use a blending mode, the top layer determines the appearance of the image – if you reverse the layers and use the same blending mode, you can get very different results.

6 The HSL influencing group: looks at colour (Hue + Saturation) and luminosity (lightness/darkness) and divides influences between the top layer and the underlying layers.

- Hue: takes only the hues (e.g. red, orange, yellow, green, blue) from the top layer and combines them with the saturation and luminosity values from the underlying layers.
- Saturation: the saturation values of the top layer are applied to the hue and luminosity of the underlying layers.
- Color: the combined hue and saturation of the top layer are assigned the luminosity values of the underlying layers.
- Luminosity: the light/dark values of the top layer are applied to the colour (hue + saturation) of the underlying layers.

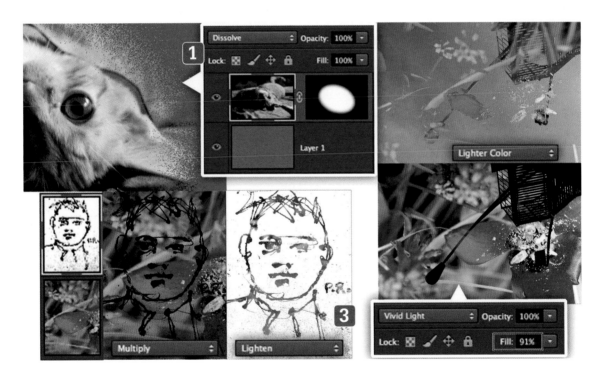

▶ SEE ALSO: When you blend layers by reducing opacity, the result often lacks contrast. You can add a curves adjustment layer to add more 'pop' to the image. See Chapter 10 for more.

Reorder layers and use Blend If

The stacking order of layers often makes a difference when blending layers or arranging elements in a digital collage. Drag layers up or down in the Layers panel to change their order. Photoshop will outline a group or thicken the line between layers to indicate where the layer will land if you release the mouse button.

In the Blending Options dialogue, the Blend If sliders mix layers based on lightness and darkness. The sliders labelled This Layer make highlights or shadows in the top layer disappear. Use the Underlying Layer sliders to force shadows or highlights up through the top layer. In the example, the Blend If Gray option was used to make the silhouetted shape invisible, showing the floral elements from beneath. Then the highlights in the red channel of the underlying layer were pushed through.

1 To use Blending Options, select Blending Options from the Layer style menu (*fx* icon) at the bottom of the Layers panel.

2 Move the sliders in the section marked This Layer to knock out parts of the top image.

3 Move the sliders in the section marked Underlying Layer to force them through the top layer.

4 Hold down the Option | Alt key and click either side of a slider to split it. Once split, you can drag the halves independently. This feathers the transition of the effect.

5 To blend based on a colour channel, select one of the channels from the Blend If menu. Adjust the sliders separately for each channel.

6 To reset the dialogue, hold down the Option | Alt key. The Cancel button will convert to a Reset button. Click the button, then release the Option | Alt key.

7 Click OK to apply the Layer style.

8 An icon appears in the Layers panel to indicate when Blending Options have been applied. Double-click the icon or select Blending Options from the *fx* menu to revise your settings.

9 To clear a Layer style (including Blend If), Control-click | Right-click on the layer name (not the thumbnail) in the Layers panel to display a menu. Select Clear Layer Style from the menu.

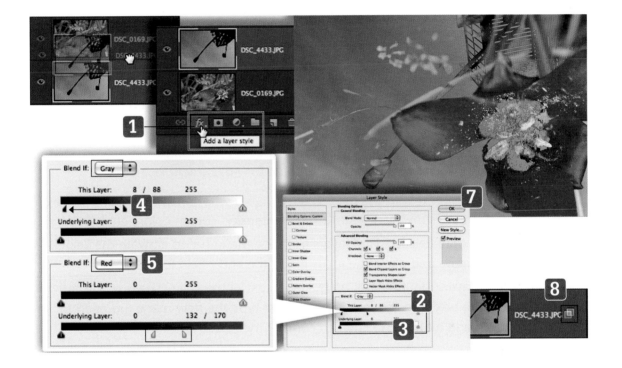

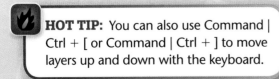

HOT TIP: You can also use Command | Ctrl + [or Command | Ctrl +] to move layers up and down with the keyboard.

Manage, find and filter layers

It's possible to build up complex Photoshop documents that contain dozens of layers and groups. That can make it challenging to locate a layer when you need to revise it. Until Photoshop CS6, naming and labelling your layers and groups was helpful – you could visually identify what you were looking for as you scrolled through the Layers panel – but only so far. Now, a suite of search capabilities built into the top of the Layers panel can filter its content in a number of ways.

1 Use the filter type menu at the top left corner of the panel to select a method for your search.

2 The filter bar has an on/off switch that turns red once you've entered criteria. You can use it to toggle the filter off and back on without losing your settings.

3 Filter by Kind: click one or more of the icons to view Pixel, Adjustment, Type, Shape or Smart Object layers. The example is filtering for Adjustment layers.

4 Filter by Name: enter text in the field to select layers whose name contains the text, e.g. enter 'beam' to show 'raw beam', 'beam intensify', 'beam color', etc.

- Shortcut: choose Select > Find layers from the menu bar to activate the Search by Name feature and place the focus inside the entry field for you.

- To rename layers: double-click on the label text of the layer. The text will convert to an editing box with the text selected. Just type the new name (no need to backspace) and hit Return | Enter to commit the text.

5 Filter by Effect: locate layers that have Effect styles applied: Drop Shadow, Outer Glow, Stroke, etc.

6 Filter by Blending mode: e.g. find all the Soft Light layers.

7 Filter by Attribute: e.g. not visible, has a layer mask, uses advanced blending (Blend If), etc.

8 Filter by Color: you can Control-click | Right-click on a layer to assign colour codes from the contextual menu that appears and then filter layers in the panel with this option.

Select, link, nudge, bump and align layers with the Move tool

You can drag, nudge or bump one or more layers with the Move tool. You can use a keystroke to switch to the tool and change its settings in the Options bar or invoke the tool temporarily by holding down a modifier key.

1 To select layers via the Layers panel:

- Click in the panel to select the first layer.
- You can select additional layers by Shift-clicking or by Command | Control-clicking on the labels (not the thumbnails) of additional layers in the panel.
- Optional: with two or more layers selected, click the chain icon to link layers. Click any linked layer and click the chain icon to unlink it from the rest.

2 To activate the Move tool, tap V on the keyboard or click its icon in the Tools panel.

3 To auto-select layers with the Move tool:

- Tick Auto-Select and select Layer or Group in the Options bar.
- Click in the image to select a layer.
- Shift-click in the image to select additional layers.
- The on-the-fly mode will use your most recent Options bar settings.

4 To select layers with the Move tool (Auto-Select turned off):

- Control-click | Right-click in the image. Any layers beneath the point where you click will appear in a menu. Choose a layer from the menu to select it.
- To select additional layers, hold down the Shift key as you Control-click | Right-click in the image and select another layer.

! ALERT: Be careful – it's easy to accidentally knock your layers out of alignment by pressing the Command | Ctrl key while painting with one of the Brush tools.

5 To use the Move tool on the fly:

- Hold down the Command | Ctrl key to temporarily convert most tools to the Move tool (the Move tool cursor will appear). Press down the mouse button and drag to move the currently selected layers. When you release the key, the tool reverts to whatever was previously active.

- When Auto-Select is off, you can hold down the Command | Ctrl key and then Control-click | Right-click to select elements as in step 4.

6 Once one or more layers are selected, you can press down the mouse button and drag in the image to reposition them. When you select a group, all its layers will move together. Linked layers also move together, even if only one of the linked items is selected.

7 To nudge the selected layers one pixel at a time, tap the arrow keys.

8 To bump the selected layers ten pixels at a time, hold down the Shift key and tap the arrow keys.

9 With two or more layers selected, you can click the icons in the Options bar to automatically align or distribute layers.

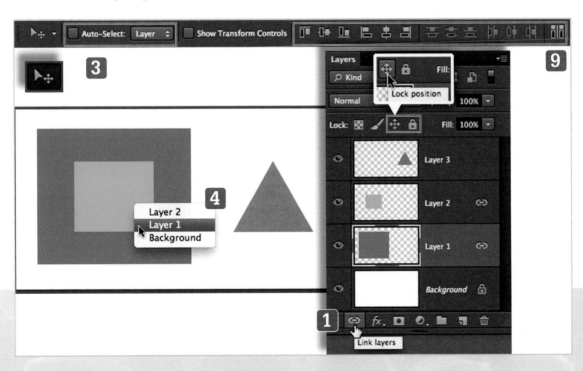

Toggle layer visibility and use layer comps

You can toggle the visibility of layers to see whether there is more to do – weaking a curve or masking an edge, for example. In some cases, you will want to turn off several layers or evaluate different combinations of layers. Layer Comps give you a one-click means of switching between different versions of your image by showing or hiding layers and layer styles or by changing the position of elements within layers. If you don't see the Layer Comps panel, select Window, Layer Comps from the menu bar.

1 To hide or show a group of layers, hold down the mouse button on the first eyeball to toggle it and drag across several others. All the layers will switch on or off to match the state of the first eyeball.

2 To isolate a layer, Option | Alt-click on the eyeball icon of the layer you want to see. All other layers will be hidden. Option | Alt-click on the same eyeball again to redisplay the other layers.

3 To create a Layer Comp:
- Click the New Layer Comp icon and enter a name.
- By default, the comp will record the visibility of the layers. Set the position and layer style options or enter a comment as required.
- Click OK to save the comp.

4 To apply a Layer Comp, click the box to the left of its label. An icon will appear to indicate that the comp is active.

5 If you add layers or want to change the visibility of layers in a Comp after you have created it, click on the Layer Comp in the panel to activate it, change the visibility settings as required, then click the Update Layer Comp button at the bottom of the panel.

6 To edit the definition of a layer comp, Control-click | Right-click on its label and choose Layer Comp Options from the menu that appears.

7 To delete a layer comp, click a text label to select it without activating and then click the trashcan icon at the bottom of the panel.

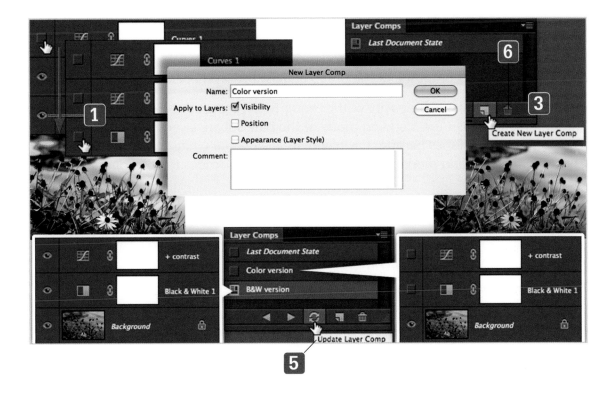

Use groups

You can create groups with a keystroke, and once created, you can easily add, remove or rearrange layers. Groups can also contain other groups, nested several levels deep. You can select a group and treat its contents as a unit or independently adjust the position, opacity and blending modes of its layers. The Pass Through blending mode is the default for groups, which means that the group has no effect on how layers within the group blend with layers beneath it. When you change the blending mode of the group to anything else, the blending modes of its layers apply only within the group. Photoshop blends a composite of the group against the layers below.

In the example shown, the opacity of the group is first reduced to 50% in Pass Through mode. When the blending mode of the blue square layer inside is changed to Color Burn, it vanishes because it is blending against the white background layer. Changing the blending mode of the group to Normal overrides the blending mode of the blue square layer.

1 To create a group:

- Click the New Group icon at the bottom of the Layers panel to create an empty group. Any selected layers will not be included.

- Select one or more layers and drag them to the New Group icon (or use Command | Ctrl + G) to create a group containing the selected layers.

2 Click the disclosure triangle to show or hide the group's contents and click the eyeball icon to toggle the group's visibility.

3 Select a group and adjust its opacity setting or blending mode as you would a layer.

4 To add layers or groups, drag the item to the group:

- If the group is expanded, you can place the item anywhere within the group. A line will appear to indicate where it will land if you release the mouse button.

- If the group is collapsed, a box will appear around the group. Your item will be placed at the bottom of the group.

5. To change the stacking order, drag layers or groups up or down in the Layers panel. You can rearrange items inside the group or move the entire group up and down within the layer stack.

6. To move a layer independently, select a layer within the group and activate the Move tool (Auto-Select set to Layer or unticked). Drag or use the arrow keys.

7. To move grouped layers together, select the group and activate the Move tool (Auto-Select set to Group or unticked). Drag or use the arrow keys.

8. To remove layers: Expand the group. Drag layers to a drop point outside the group, then release the mouse button. (If a group is sitting immediately above the background, you won't be able to drag layers out of the bottom.)

9. To remove all layers from a group and discard the group folder, Control-click | Right-click on the group's label and choose Ungroup Layers from the menu. (You'll get a different menu if you Control-click | Right-click on the folder icon.)

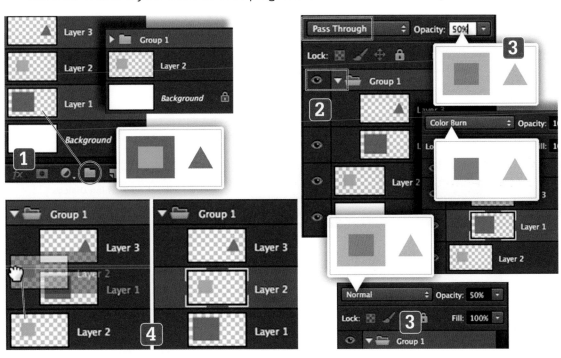

Delete a layer or group

All the methods listed below will delete one or more layers or groups at the same time. Use the methods mentioned earlier to select layers, groups or a mix of both, and then delete in one of the following ways:

1 Hit the Delete | Backspace key to delete the item(s) immediately.

2 Drag the item(s) to the trashcan icon at the bottom of the Layers panel to delete immediately.

3 Click the trashcan icon at the bottom of the Layers panel.

- Optional: if you see a confirmation dialogue, you can tick Don't show again (to avoid these messages in the future) before confirming.

- Click Yes to confirm.

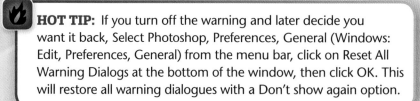

HOT TIP: If you turn off the warning and later decide you want it back, Select Photoshop, Preferences, General (Windows: Edit, Preferences, General) from the menu bar, click on Reset All Warning Dialogs at the bottom of the window, then click OK. This will restore all warning dialogues with a Don't show again option.

Merge, stamp or flatten layers

Selectively merging layers in your file can simplify its structure and reduce file size. Stamping a layer is helpful when you want to apply filters (e.g. for sharpening) to images that contain adjustment layers. Flattening can save file space and speed printing sometimes, but it cannot be undone once you save and close a file. After flattening, you can step back in the History panel to restore the layers to your file and continue working with it, or you can use the Save As command to store a flattened copy alongside your layered original (e.g. image3250.psd and image3250_print.psd).

1 To merge down, select a layer and use Command | Ctrl + E to merge it with the layer immediately beneath. When you select a group, this command merges all the contents of the group.

2 To merge layers, select two or more layers and choose Layer, Merge Layers (Command | Ctrl + E) from the menu bar.

3 To stamp a layer:
- Select the topmost layer in your file and click the Add a new layer icon.
- Rename the new blank layer as required.
- While holding the Option | Alt key, select Merge Visible from the menu in the upper right corner of the Layers panel.
- If layers disappear, you released the Option | Alt key too soon. Use Undo and then try again.

4 To flatten, choose Layer, Flatten Image from the menu bar.

5 The Merge Layers, Merge Down, Merge Visible and Flatten Image commands are all available via the fly-out menu in the upper right corner of the Layers panel.

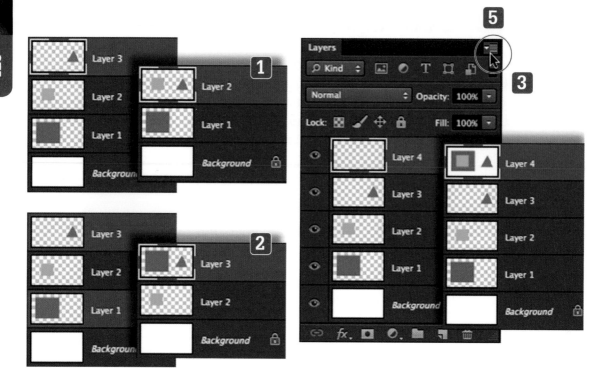

8 View, zoom and navigate

Introduction

An array of viewing tools allows you to quickly unclutter your screen, work at different magnifications and move around the image easily, even when working at high magnification. However, a number of these features rely on the graphics processor built into your computer's video card. Older video cards do not support the necessary graphics library.

To confirm whether your computer supports them, select Photoshop, Preferences, Performance (Windows: Edit, Preferences, Performance) from the menu bar and look at the Graphics Processor Settings section. If you are unable to tick the box marked Use Graphics Processor, your video card does not support it. Unticking the option will disable many of the features in this chapter and others found throughout this book.

Zoom in or out and move around in your image

Whenever you need to work on fine detail in your image, you can zoom in. At other times you'll want to zoom out to take in the entire image. Photoshop has several keystrokes and tools to adjust magnification. When you zoom into more than 500%, a grid appears to show individual pixels. You have the option to turn off this feature.

1. Hold down Command | Ctrl and press the plus sign or the minus sign to zoom in or out incrementally.

2. Use Command | Ctrl + 1 to zoom in to 100% (i.e. each pixel in your image fills one pixel onscreen).

3. Use Command | Ctrl + 0 (zero) or double-click the Hand tool button in the Tools panel to fit the image in the window.

4. To zoom to a specific percentage, click in the size box at the lower left corner of the image, enter a value and hit Return | Enter.

5. Tap the Z key to switch to the Zoom tool or hold the Z key to use the Zoom tool on the fly and revert to the previous tool when you release the key.
   - With the Scrubby Zoom box ticked, drag to the right to zoom in and drag to the left to zoom out.
   - You can also use the buttons in the Options bar to set the Zoom level. Actual Pixels = 100%.

6. Use the Hand tool to move around in the image. Hold the space bar to temporarily engage the Hand tool or tap the H key to switch to the tool.
   - Use the buttons in the Options bar to set the Zoom level.
   - Drag in the image with the Hand tool to reposition the view.

- You can also use Flick Panning: hold down the mouse button, snap your wrist and release the mouse button to glide the image to a new location. You can stop the glide by clicking the mouse button again.

[7] To use Bird's Eye View, hold down the H key and then hold down the mouse button. The image will zoom out. Drag the rectangular outline to a new location and then release the mouse button. The image will zoom back into the new location. Release the H key to revert to the previous tool.

[8] To toggle the pixel grid, select View, Show, Pixel Grid. A tick appears in the menu when the feature is active.

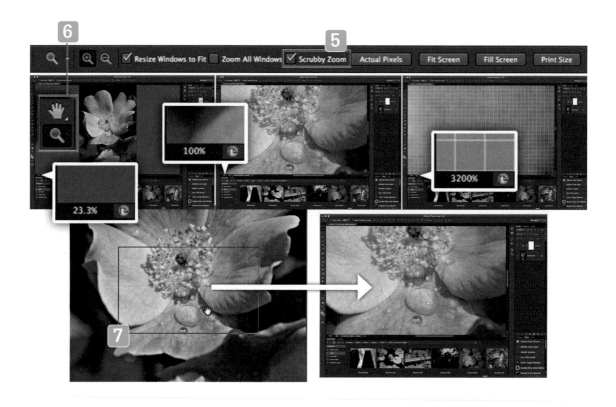

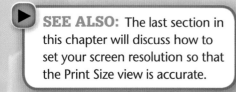

SEE ALSO: The last section in this chapter will discuss how to set your screen resolution so that the Print Size view is accurate.

Work with screen modes and composition aids

Sometimes, Photoshop's panels can be in the way, but there are a number of ways you can resize or hide them, including three screen modes. In full-screen mode, the panels are hidden along with the menu bar for maximum viewing area. In standard-screen mode, the image is locked in place whenever the entire image fits on screen, but in either of the full-screen modes you can hold down the space bar to drag the image around the viewing area. For precise positioning, you can use guides, grids, rulers and Snap.

1 Tap the F key repeatedly to cycle through the screen modes or use the screen mode icon in the Tools panel.

2 Hit the Tab key to show or hide all panels, regardless of screen mode.

3 Use Shift + Tab to hide or show just the panels on the right and bottom.

4 When the panels are hidden, hover the mouse pointer over the left, right or bottom edge of the screen to reveal a panel. It will snap back when you move the cursor away.

5 To show rulers, use Command | Ctrl + R or select View, Rulers from the menu bar.
   - To change the ruler scale, Control-click | Right-click on one of the rulers and select a new scale from the menu.
   - Press the mouse button down on a ruler and drag to manually place new guides. You can reposition guides with the Move tool.

6 To toggle the Smart Guides feature, select View, Show, Smart Guides. The feature dynamically draws lines to indicate relationships between elements of your composition as you drag them.

7 To toggle the Grid display, select View, Show, Grid from the menu bar.

- To adjust grids and guides, select Photoshop, Preferences, Guides, Grid and Slices (Windows: Edit, Preferences, Guides, Grid and Slices) from the menu bar.

8 Select View, Snap to toggle the feature. When ticked, objects will gravitate to Guides, Grids, Layers, etc. as you drag them with the Move tool. It can also help you paint straight lines along guides or gridlines. You can use the View, Snap To menu to control what items will snap.

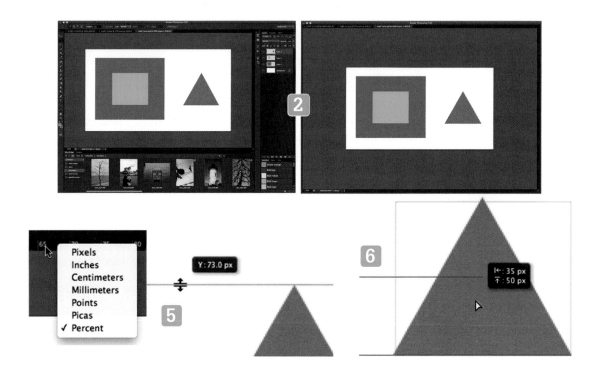

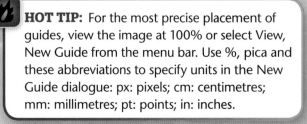

HOT TIP: For the most precise placement of guides, view the image at 100% or select View, New Guide from the menu bar. Use %, pica and these abbreviations to specify units in the New Guide dialogue: px: pixels; cm: centimetres; mm: millimetres; pt: points; in: inches.

Hide or show extras and calculate your screen resolution

Guides, grids and 'marching ant' selections are examples of Extras, items which help you edit your image, but do not appear in prints or exported files. You can switch Extras on or off individually or as a group.

The View, Print Size command will work well only if you enter a resolution more accurate than the default screen resolution of 72 dpi. You can enter 100 dpi as a better default, since most screens today range between about 95 and 120 dpi, or you can calculate your actual resolution. The process is outlined beginning with step 5.

1 To show or hide all Extras, select View, Extras (Command | Ctrl + H) from the menu bar or by selecting View, Show, All or View, Show, None from the menu bar.

2 Pull down the View, Show menu to see which ones are active. A tick appears next to active Extras.

3 Select an item from the View, Show menu to toggle individual Extras.

4 To enable or disable multiple Extras in one shot, select View, Show, Show Extras Options from the menu bar to display a dialogue.

5 To determine your screen size in pixels, locate your computer's display settings and write down the active dimensions. The dimensions are given as width × height.

- On a Mac, look for the Displays icon in your menu bar. Click to display your screen dimensions.

- If you don't see the Displays icon: a) select System Preferences from the Apple menu; b) click Displays; c) click Displays in the navigation bar at the top; d) your screen dimensions will be highlighted.

- On Windows 7, open Screen Resolution: a) click the Start button; b) click Control Panel; c) under Appearance and Personalization, click Adjust screen resolution.

- Open Display Settings: a) click the Start button; b) click Control Panel; c) click Appearance and Personalization; d) click Personalization; e) click Display Settings.

6 Measure the width of the actual image on your screen. You won't need both dimensions. Be careful not to scratch your display.

7 To calculate your resolution, divide the pixel width by the inches or centimetres you measured. For the iMac in this example, 2560 pixels/23.5 inches = 109 pixels/inch.

8 To enter your resolution, select Photoshop, Preferences, Units & Rulers (Windows: Edit, Preferences, Units & Rulers) from the menu bar. In the section labelled New Document Preset Resolutions, enter the value you just calculated into the Screen Resolution field.

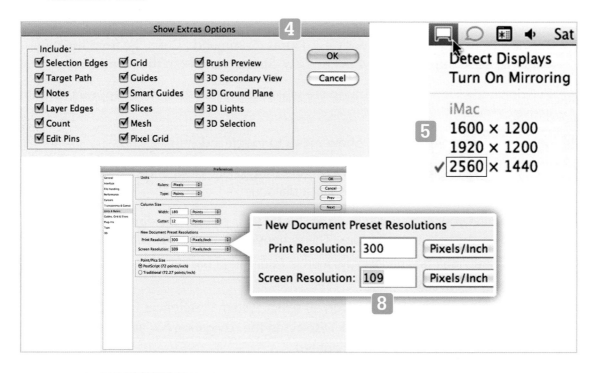

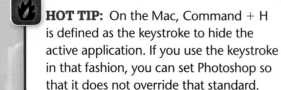

HOT TIP: On the Mac, Command + H is defined as the keystroke to hide the active application. If you use the keystroke in that fashion, you can set Photoshop so that it does not override that standard.

9 Work with brushes

Introduction

When you need to modify a mask, you're likely to use the Brush tool in its simplest way: tap the B key to activate it, select a soft (Hardness = 0) round brush and start to paint. In some cases, you might also use Opacity, Flow and possibly Airbrush-style build-up, but this hardly scratches the surface of what you can do creatively with Photoshop's brushes. Some can simulate the way bristles deform as you press and tilt your brush, and erodible tips introduced in Photoshop CS6 wear down as you draw, the way real-life materials like charcoal do. New airbrush tips not only emulate spraying and spattering paint effects but can also simulate watercolour.

These features expand the possibilities for making images well beyond basic photo editing and they are all based on Photoshop's brush 'engine'. Not only does it power the Brush tool (and tools with the word brush in them), but also the Pencil, Clone Stamp, Eraser and several more. Once you learn to use the Brush tool, you'll find that many of its characteristics and options (such as opacity and painting modes) carry over to other brush-based tools.

Understanding brushes

When you paint in Photoshop, you apply patterns of pixels to a layer. Those patterns can form a recognisable repeating shape or something scattered and highly randomised; it all depends upon the brush tip (which defines the basic shape of the brush marks) and settings such as Shape Dynamics, Scattering and Texture. The colour of the marks depends upon the foreground and sometimes the background colour.

1. Set the colours – you can tap D to select the defaults. Tap X to swap foreground and background. You can also use the Color panel or click the swatches in the Tools panel to open the colour picker.

2. Click a button in the Options bar or Control-click | Right-click in the image to open the Brush picker. You can use it to select a brush, change Size and Hardness, and save your brush along with its settings as a preset.

3. For a gradual build-up effect, you can reduce the opacity of your strokes via the Options bar.

4. The Flow and Airbrush-style build-up controls offer additional methods for applying colour gradually.

5. You can toggle icons in the Options panel to control opacity and brush size with a graphics tablet.

6. Clicking the folder icon in the Options bar opens the Brush panel, the command centre for defining brushes. You can modify your current brush or transfer its settings to a different brush tip to create a new brush.

7. A button in the Brush panel opens the Brush Presets panel, which you can use to select a brush (tip + settings) to be modified in the Brush panel. You can then click a button to switch back to the Brush panel, where you can finish creating a new brush.

8. You can save the current brush as a preset from the Brush picker, the Brush Presets panel or the Brush panel.

9 Tool Presets work like Brush Presets, but also record attributes such as colour, opacity and flow (e.g. an orange 25-pixel erodible crayon). Click the icon at the left edge of the Options bar to display the Tool Preset picker and use it to select an existing preset or save your brush settings as a new Tool Preset.

10 The Preset Manager allows you to control a potentially overwhelming array of presets. Menus in the Brush Preset picker and Brush Preset panel allow you to load additional libraries of brushes. You can also create your own libraries and organise your brushes.

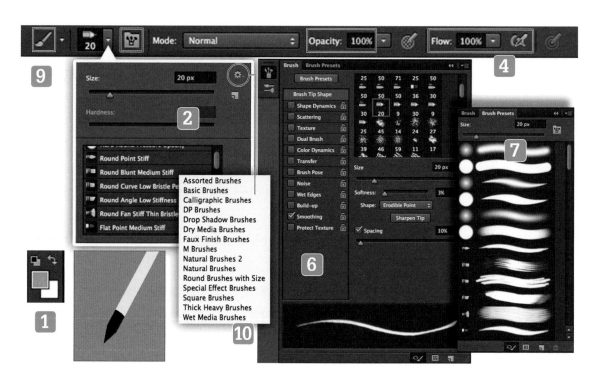

ALERT: There are two things to watch out for when using Brushes. a) When you turn on the Caps Lock key, the Brush displays its precise cursor – a simple crosshair – instead of its normal cursor. This can be confusing. b) Holding down the Command | Ctrl key converts the Brush to the Move tool. Instead of applying paint, you'll reposition the selected layer.

Use the Brush Preset picker

Once you tap the B key or click the icon in the Tools panel to activate the Brush tool, you're likely to activate the Brush Preset picker to select a brush before doing anything else. Beyond the pre-loaded brushes that appear in the picker when you install Photoshop, 15 additional libraries of brushes are available to load on demand. You can create your own libraries as well. If your list of brushes gets confusing, you can reinstate the default set and start again.

1 Click the button in the Options bar or Control-click | Right-click in the image to open the Brush Preset picker.

2 Optional: use the gear menu icon in the upper right corner of the panel to change the way brushes are listed, i.e. text, thumbnails, lists or stroke thumbnail.

3 You can click in the list to select a brush as required.

4 Use the sliders to adjust Size and Hardness as required.

5 Optional: once you change either setting, you can click the dog-eared page icon to save your settings as a new brush.

6 For more brushes, select an item from the lower portion of the fly-out menu to load additional brush sets, e.g. M Brushes.

- When you load a brush set, you'll have the option to either append the new brushes (add them to the brushes already in the list) or replace the current list with the new brushes.

7 You can choose Reset Brushes from the fly-out menu to restore the default list of brushes at any time.

8 Hit Return | Enter to close the panel.

DID YOU KNOW?

You don't have to adjust brush size in the Brush Preset picker dialogue. You can change brush size at any time by using the square bracket keys (just to the right of the P key). Tap] to make the brush larger and tap [to make it smaller. Hold the Shift key and tap the bracket keys to increase or decrease the hardness.

HOT TIP: A second way to adjust the brush settings is to hold down Control + Option and the mouse button (Windows: hold down Alt and the Right-click button), then drag horizontally to change the brush size or vertically to change the hardness.

SEE ALSO: Later in this chapter, we'll look at the Brush panel. You'll use that to modify brushes that you select from primitive brush tips or if you want to modify your brushes beyond the basic settings available in the Options bar.

Select and sample colours

The overlapping colour swatches in the Tools panel show the current foreground and background colours. The brush applies the foreground colour as you paint. The Brush tool doesn't have to be active to select the foreground and background colours, since many other tools and filters also use them.

1 Tap D to set the default colours: black foreground, white background. Tap X at any time to swap foreground and background colours.

2 Click the foreground or background swatch to open the colour picker for that swatch.

3 To use the Color Picker, click a hue in the vertical strip and then click in the box to select saturation and brightness values.

4 Click Color Libraries to select Pantone and other matching system colours. Once the dialogue is open, you can select a book from the menu and then type numbers to jump to the colour you want or scroll and click on a colour to select it. Click Picker to return to the main colour picker dialogue.

5 You can set colours numerically by entering RGB, web, HSB, CMYK or Lab values into the appropriate boxes.

6 Optional: click Add to Swatches to name and save a colour to the Swatches panel.

7 You can also set the foreground colour by clicking in the Swatches panel. Use the menu icon in the upper right corner of the panel to list the swatches in different ways. You can load sets of colour swatches in the same manner as you load brushes in the Brush Preset picker.

 HOT TIP: When the Eyedropper tool is active, the Options bar features a Sample Size menu – 3 by 3 or 5 by 5 are generally better choices to work with. Point sample is often too precise, and 11 by 11 or larger typically sample too many pixels.

8. The Color panel is an alternative to the Color Picker dialogue. You can use the menu in the upper right corner of the panel to separately configure the input sliders and the colour ramp at the bottom of the panel (e.g. HSB Sliders + Grayscale Ramp).

- Click one of the swatches on the left side of the panel to change the foreground or background colour. (If you click the active swatch a second time, the Color Picker dialogue will open. You can click Cancel.)

- Click on the ramp, enter numerical values, or move the sliders to select a colour.

9. Photoshop also has several ways to sample colour from the image. If you use the Color panel, the selected swatch will determine whether the sampled colour is assigned to the foreground or the background. Photoshop's default behaviour is to assign the sampled colour to the foreground.

- When the Brush tool is active, you can hold down the Option | Alt key and click in the image to sample colour from the image.

- When any tool is active, hold the I key to temporarily invoke the Eyedropper tool. Click in the image to sample colour. Release the I key to return to the previously active tool. You can also switch to the Eyedropper by tapping the letter I.

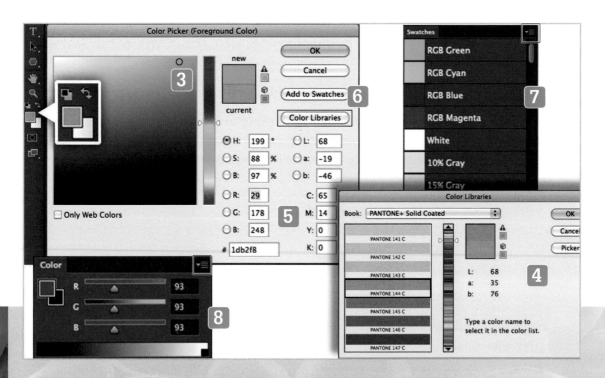

Build up colour gradually

When you need to build up colour gradually, you can use the Brush tool in its normal mode with reduced opacity and 100% Flow, or you can also reduce the Flow. Switch on Airbrush-style build-up for additional options. When the hardness setting of the brush is high, reducing Opacity tends to work better than reducing Flow. When the hardness is low, reducing the Flow can produce more subtle effects.

1. Opacity determines the density of colour that will be applied in one stroke or click of the mouse. (A stroke consists of pressing down the mouse button, dragging and releasing the mouse button.) At a 50% opacity setting, you'll need to release the mouse button, press it again and go over the same area to exceed 50% opacity in that area.

2. Flow controls how quickly colour is applied. If you combine low Flow (e.g. 5%) with 100% opacity and leave Airbrush-style build-up off, you can hold down the mouse button and go over the same area repeatedly to gradually build colour all the way up to 100% density without releasing the mouse button. While you don't have to release the mouse button, you do have to move the mouse.

3. When you switch on Airbrush-style build-up and press down the mouse button, the opacity of your colour will build, even if you don't move the brush around. That means you'll need to keep your hand moving if you want a smooth application of colour.

4. When you combine Opacity with Flow, your strokes will gradually build to the maximum Opacity before you have to release the mouse button and start a new stroke. The result can be smooth and subtle gradations of tone.

5. With Airbrush-style build-up switched off, tap 0 for 100% opacity and 1–9 for 10% to 90% respectively. Tap two digits quickly to set values like 25 or 75. Hold down the Shift key and tap digits to set the Flow. When Airbrush-style build-up is on, tap digits to affect Flow and Shift + digits to affect Opacity.

? DID YOU KNOW?

Photoshop CS6 includes pressure- and tilt-sensitive Airbrush tips (available via the Brush Preset picker and Brush panels). These are distinct from Airbrush-style build-up, which you can use with most types of brush tips.

Reshape brushes

Aside from adjusting the size, opacity and flow of a brush, there will be times when you'll want to alter its shape. You can do that in the Brush panel and even save your altered brush as a preset for future use. There are four major types of brushes in Photoshop, each with different shaping options. Photoshop's basic brushes have been a staple of the software for a long time. Three newer tip designs are essentially virtual brushes that work best with a graphics tablet because they model the effects of pressure and tilt. A live preview indicates how these brushes are oriented in virtual space and how their shape is changing in response to the stylus.

1 To reveal the brush shape controls, select Window, Brush from the menu bar (tap the F5 key) to display the Brush panel and then click Brush Tip Shape at the top of the list on the left side.

2 Basic brushes: these include round, spatter and shape brushes such as Scattered Leaves. Dual brushes like Wet Sponge combine two basic brush tips, one masking the other. You can make round brushes oval and set the angle of the brush.

3 Erodible tips: new to this version of Photoshop, these tips have three-dimensional forms that wear down and change shape as you use them. Select from pointed, flat, round, square, triangular and custom shapes. Changing the Softness setting determines how quickly the tip erodes. Click Sharpen Tip to restore the brush to its original shape.

4 Bristle tips: introduced in CS5, the stroke of a Bristle tip brush can change dramatically depending on how you press and tilt the stylus. You can select from five tip shapes and alter the bristles five ways.

5 Airbrush tips: also new to CS6, these brushes can emulate the effect of spraying paint and the application of watercolour. These tips have several adjustable parameters, including Hardness, Distortion and Spatter Amount.

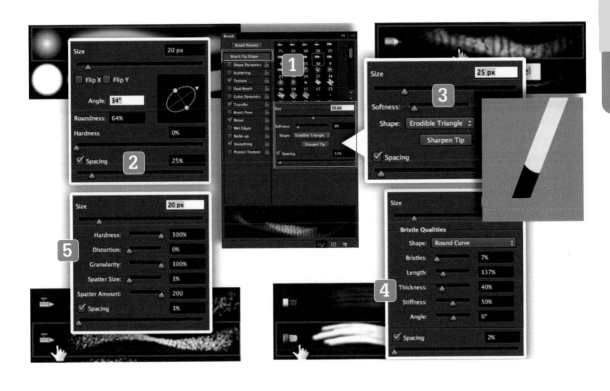

Use the Brush and Brush Presets panels

The Brush panel is also your workshop for constructing brushes. Its companion, the Brush Presets panel, is slightly different from the Brush picker in the Options bar and affords a way to build new brushes from saved presets.The combination of a brush tip and its settings constitutes a brush. A vertical strip of tick boxes on the left side of the Brush panel manages settings, and you can select a brush tip from the box on the right.

1 Tap B to activate the Brush tool and the Brush panel controls. If you don't see the panel, select Window, Brush from the menu bar. The panel will open with the settings for the current brush. Click Brush Tip Shape at the top of the list on the left side to display its controls.

2 To apply the settings of the current brush to a different tip, click on a new tip in the picker pane in the upper right portion of the panel (you can hover the cursor over a thumbnail to see a description). To switch to the Brush Presets panel and select a different brush as a starting point, click Brush Presets.

3 In the Brush Presets panel, you can use the menu in the upper right corner to change the way it displays brushes, load and save additional brush libraries, or reset your brushes to the default library.

- Click a thumbnail in the Brush Presets panel to select it.
- Click the lock icon to hold settings from the current brush and apply them to other brushes you select in the Brush Presets panel.
- Click the Brush panel icon at the top of the panel to return from the Brush Presets panel.

4 In the Brush panel, use the list on the left side and the corresponding controls on the lower right to reconfigure the brush. The stroke preview at the bottom will update as you make changes. A tapered stroke preview indicates that the size of the brush is controlled by pen pressure.

- Click the labels of the items with a line above and below (Shape Dynamics through to Brush Pose) to tick the box and display its controls. Click the box on these items to toggle the tick.
- Click either the label or the box to toggle Noise, Wet Edges, Build-up, Smoothing and Protect Texture.

5 To save a new brush, click the dog-eared page icon at the bottom of either pane and enter a name into the dialogue. When you click OK, the brush will be added to the end of your list of brushes.

6 To delete a brush, Option | Alt-click on it or select it and click the bin icon at the bottom of the panel.

7 To reorganise your brushes, click the Preset Manager button at the bottom of either panel.

- Drag brushes in the dialogue to reorder them. You can select multiple brushes and drag them together.
- You can also use the gear menu in the upper right to change the appearance of your brush lists and manage brush sets.
- Click Done to exit the dialogue and save your changes.

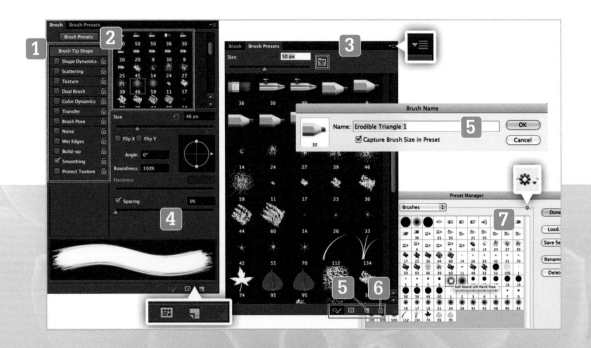

Use a graphics tablet and brush pose

Whenever you activate the Brush tool, two icons in the Options bar hint at a broad range of functionality that is available when you attach a graphics tablet to your computer. They allow you to override the Brush panel settings and use pressure to control opacity and brush size. Drawing and painting with a stylus instead of a mouse also feels a lot more like working with pens, pencils and brushes. If you don't have a graphics tablet, Photoshop CS6 introduces a feature called Brush Pose that provides some of that functionality when working with a mouse or trackpad.

A graphics tablet consists of a flat control surface with a pen-like stylus. One of the best tablets on the market is the Wacom Intuos 4. Its standard Grip Pen allows you to control Photoshop features by varying how hard you press the stylus to the tablet surface or by tilting the stylus. With the Art Pen, you can also control various features by rotating the barrel of the pen.

1. The Shape Dynamics, Scattering, Texture, Color Dynamics and Transfer settings in the Brush Panel all have controls that can be driven by a tablet.

2. Bristle tips, Erodible tips and Airbrush tips all rely heavily on both pressure and tilt. Without the Brush Pose feature, they're virtually useless with a mouse.

3. The Intuos 4 has a programmable rocker switch on the body of the stylus and a set of programmable controls on the tablet itself. Its Grip Pen does not register rotation, but you can emulate that to some degree with Brush Pose.

4. You can also use Brush Pose to lock in tilt, rotation or pressure by overriding the tablet's input.

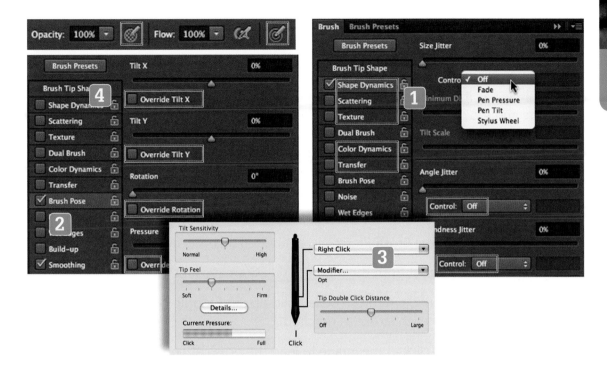

Use the Mixer Brush

The Mixer Brush is nested beneath the Brush tool in the Tools panel. It allows you to treat an image as if it's wet paint. You can use any brush tip with the Mixer Brush, but the bristle and erodible tips are particularly good for this application.

1 Add an empty layer at the top of your Layers panel.

2 Activate the Mixer Brush in the Tools panel.

3 Tick Sample All Layers in the Options bar.

4 Select a brush from the Brush Preset picker and refine as needed in the Brush panel.

5 Choose a mixture preset from the menu or set parameters for Wet, Load and Mix.

6 Optional: set Flow, enable Airbrush-style build-up, and toggle options to load or clean the brush after each stroke as required.

7 You can Option | Alt-click in the image to load the brush at any time.

8 You can also use the Brush Load menu (next to the Brush panel icon) to load solid colours only and to clean the brush.

HOT TIP: Because colour from the brush can mix with colours already in the image, you can sample and mix colours on a blank part of the document or in a separate window the way you would on a painter's palette, then sample those colours to paint in the image.

10 Adjust colour and tone

Introduction

In this chapter, we will explore techniques for adjusting tones and colours in an image. Photoshop has three fundamentally different ways of altering colour and tone. First, you can change the colour and tone of pixels directly by applying commands, filters or tools to a pixel layer. Second, you can use blending modes. However, you're likely to use the third method the most: you can add non-destructive adjustment layers, which alter the appearance of the layers that they sit above without modifying the pixels in those layers.

Each type of adjustment layer has an equivalent command in the Image, Adjustments menu (e.g. Image, Adjustments, Curves is the command form of Layer, New Adjustment Layer, Curves). You permanently alter the pixels in a layer when you apply the command form of an adjustment, so it's usually best to apply such direct adjustments (also referred to as destructive adjustments) to duplicate layers, stamped layers, smart objects or masks.

Use adjustment layers

Adjustment layers alter the appearance of your image, but encapsulate that alteration in a layer that you can toggle on and off, rather than directly altering the pixels in the layers that sit beneath it. An adjustment layer appears as a thumbnail in the Layers panel and you adjust its settings via the Properties panel, which is new to Photoshop CS6. There are 19 different types of tonal and colour adjustments that you can make to your image with adjustment layers, and a few are likely to be everyday staples. The example shows an image adjusted with a Curves adjustment to add contrast and a Vibrance adjustment, which makes colours more intense without over-saturating them.

1. To add an adjustment layer, click in the Layers panel to select a layer and select an item from the menu under the black and white circle icon. The new adjustment layer will be placed immediately above the previously selected layer and the new layer will be selected.

2. The controls for the selected adjustment layer will appear in the Properties panel. If you don't see the Properties panel, you can double-click the thumbnail of an adjustment layer to reveal the panel.

3. To enable or disable an adjustment, just toggle its visibility. Click the eyeball icon at the bottom of the Properties panel or on the left edge of the Layers panel – they are equivalent.

4. Besides adjusting parameters in the Properties panel, you can reduce the opacity of an adjustment layer to reduce its strength, and you can change the blending mode of the adjustment for a range of effects.

5. To apply an adjustment to a specific area of an image: adjustment layers automatically include a layer mask that you can paint in shades of grey to control where the adjustment is applied. The black areas of the mask hide the adjustment completely, while shades of grey let some of the effect through. The effect is in full force wherever the mask is white.

6 You can also clip an adjustment to the layer immediately beneath it to create what is known as a clipping mask. When you do that, the adjustment affects only the layer it is clipped to. You can click a button at the bottom of the Properties panel or click in the Layers panel to create or release a clipping mask.

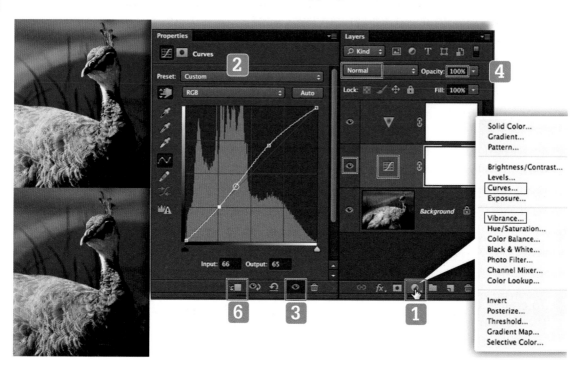

? **DID YOU KNOW?**

You can also add adjustment layers by selecting from the Layer, New Adjustment Layer menu or by clicking on one of the icons in the Adjustments panel.

Adjust tonality

Photoshop has several adjustments that can be applied to alter tonality, which is the assortment of light and dark values within an image. As you adjust your images, you'll often think in terms of blacks, shadows, midtones, highlights and whites. The adjustments work by lightening or darkening tones based on their initial values (Photoshop calls them levels). The Histogram panel is useful for visualising the distribution of tones in your image as you make your adjustments. It can indicate when you've forced certain tones to black or white and lost detail, a condition known as clipping. Shadows that have been clipped are said to be 'blocked up' and clipped highlights are often said to be 'blown out'.

1 Brightness/Contrast: the simplest of the adjustments. It has only two sliders that are pretty self-explanatory. The contrast adjustment essentially focuses on middle tones, pushing the shadows and highlights apart as you increase contrast.

2 Exposure: this slider is measured in stops that correspond to how exposure works in your camera, making your overall image lighter or darker. Gamma Correction focuses more on the middle tones and has a different effect. Offset focuses on the shadows and can quickly turn your shadows to blocked-up ink or washed-out haze. Instead of using the sliders, click in the value box and use the up or down arrow keys to move the values gradually. Use Shift + an arrow key to move in larger increments.

3 Levels is a popular adjustment because it uses simple sliders, but it's essentially been made obsolete by Curves. Its main controls are sliders for gamma adjustment (making the image lighter or darker), black point (for images where there are no pure blacks) and white point (for images where the whites are actually grey). The Output Levels controls can lighten pure blacks and darken pure whites.

4 Curves can do everything that Levels can do, plus it can produce a range of contrast effects that Levels cannot match. If you understand how to use Curves, it's no more difficult to use than Levels. The Curves adjustment also has an option to point and drag inside the image to lighten or darken tones.

5. Auto toning: Brightness/Contrast, Levels and Curves all have an Auto button that works well to adjust tonality in your image. They each produce different results because they work differently.

6. Droppers: Exposure, Levels and Curves all have a trio of dropper controls. You activate a dropper and click in the image to sample and set the black point, white point and grey point (similar to white balance). These tools are somewhat useful, but also problematic.

7. To display the Histogram panel, select Window, Histogram from the menu bar.

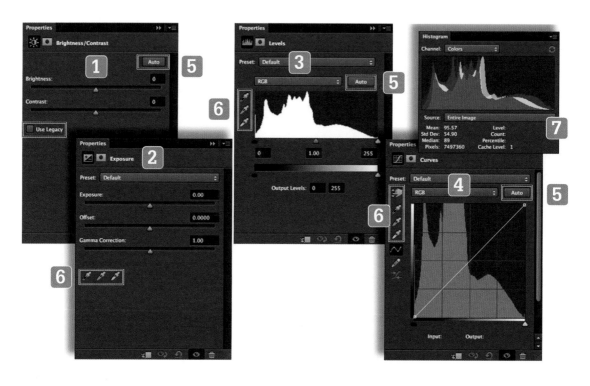

Use Curves with auto or preset options

The Curves adjustment is versatile and powerful, so we'll spend some time with it in this and the next two sections. Two of the easiest ways to use Curves are essentially automatic. Just add the adjustment layer and click a button or choose a menu item.

Photoshop CS6 includes a new Auto-toning routine that works much better than in earlier versions (they often induced unwanted colour casts and other problems). You can still get to the older routines by Option | Alt-clicking on the Auto button, but you're not likely to need them.

1. Click in the Layers panel to select a layer before you add a new Curves layer. The new adjustment layer will be added immediately above it. (If your only layer is the Background, you don't need to select it first.) Select Curves from the New Adjustment Layer menu at the bottom of the Layers panel. The Curves controls will appear in the Properties panel.

2. To adjust an existing Curves layer, double-click on the thumbnail for the layer to show its settings in the Properties panel.

3. To use auto-toning, click the Auto button in the Properties panel.

4. To use a preset curve, select an item from the Preset menu. Try other presets as required.

   - The Color Negative, Cross Process and Negative presets alter the colour dramatically. The other adjustments are essentially neutral.
   - The Negative preset does the same thing as the Invert adjustment.

5. After using the Auto button or selecting a preset, you can adjust the curve manually (more on that in the next two sections).

6 You can click the eyeball icon at the bottom of the Properties panel or in the Layers panel to toggle the adjustment and compare before and after. Click the curved arrow icon next to it to reset the panel to its defaults.

7 Use the panel menu in the upper right corner to save or load custom presets. You can copy saved preset files and load them into the Curves panel on another computer.

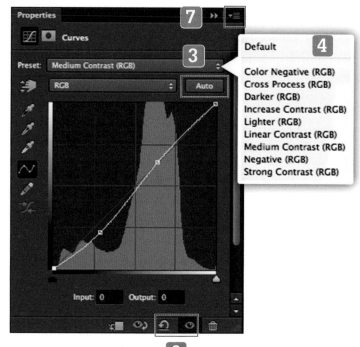

SEE ALSO: Often, you'll see the saturation increase as you increase contrast in a colour photo, and there are times where it can increase too much. You can compensate for that by adding a Hue/Saturation layer. See details later in this chapter.

HOT TIP: You can also automatically adjust tones by dragging in the image. Click the hand icon in the upper left area of the Properties panel, position the cursor over a light or dark area in the image, and press the mouse button down to select the corresponding tones in the curve. Drag up or down to reshape the curve.

Adjust the black point and white point

Photos shot on overcast days can have weak shadows, dull highlights and low contrast. You can dramatically improve such images with a Curves or Levels adjustment. Moving the black point to the right can add weight. Similarly, dull highlights can be improved by moving the white point to the left. Either of these moves makes the graph steeper in Curves, which indicates that contrast is increasing. Of course, you'll see it in the image, too. Presets will clear any settings you've already made, so you'll want to adjust the black point and white point manually (not with the droppers) afterwards if you choose a preset.

As you push the controls inwards, you'll be clipping tones: forcing tones that were previously grey to black or white. The grey ramp overlays on the example image have been added to show how the curve affects tones on the bottom. Too much clipping is not a good thing. However, you can watch out for clipping in the Histogram panel and use a modifier key to get a visual indication of clipping as you adjust the sliders.

1. Optional: select a preset to establish your basic curve.

2. To adjust the black point; drag the black triangle towards the right. You'll see the shadows darken.

3. To adjust the white point; drag the white triangle towards the left. You'll see the highlights lighten.

4. For a clipping preview, hold down the Option | Alt key as you drag the black point or white point slider. You'll typically want to move the slider to the point where colour just begins to break through and then back it off until the colour vanishes. If you can't make the colours vanish, you can leave the slider at its extreme right or left position.

5 You can compare the distribution of tones before and after the adjustment by comparing the histogram in the Properties panel to the contents of the Histogram panel. If you see an exclamation point icon in either panel, click it to refresh the display.

6 Moving the black point up creates a washed-out effect that can be good for creating images that you can use as backgrounds for graphic designs, and moving the white point down greys out the highlights. Click on either end point in the graph and drag it, or use the up and down arrow keys.

7 The Levels adjustment has different presets and fewer adjustment options, but you can adjust the black point and white point in the same fashion as above. Moving the Output Levels controls is equivalent to moving the black and white points vertically in Curves.

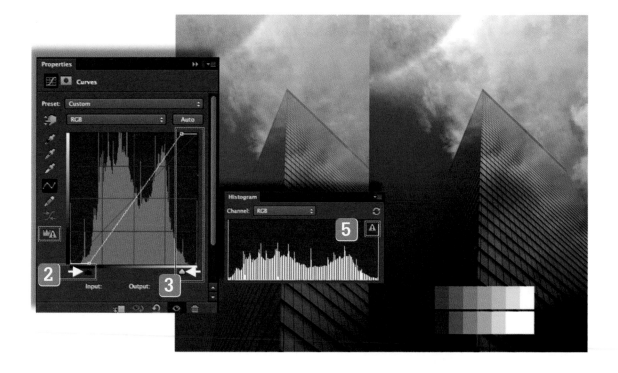

ALERT: The dropper tools can sample the black point, white point and grey point for you, but it's generally better to avoid them and manually adjust the black point and white point. They can clear settings you have already made in your curve, and you may also find that your colours shift in unsatisfactory ways.

Adjust saturation and vibrance

Saturation is the relative purity of the colours in an image. There will be times where you will want to increase or decrease the amount of saturation in an image simply for aesthetic reasons. You can adjust saturation with the Vibrance or Hue/Saturation adjustments.

1 Select Hue/Saturation or Vibrance from the New Layer menu.

2 The Hue/Saturation adjustment can sometimes boost saturation too far.

- Adjust carefully. Skin does not look good when it's overly saturated and colours can look garish when too much saturation is added.
- Avoid the Lightness setting. It generally makes images hazy or murky.

3 The Vibrance adjustment takes a more nuanced approach, protecting skin tones and limiting its saturation boost to less saturated colours.

- The Vibrance adjustment layer has its own Saturation slider, but it does not work as aggressively as the slider in the Hue/Saturation adjustment.
- A Vibrance setting of –100 still has hints of colour. Low-Vibrance images can be an interesting alternative to black and white conversion.

4 Toggle your adjustment layer on and off with the eyeball icon to evaluate the results.

−100%   +100%

Target a colour and adjust hue and saturation

In the previous section, we looked at adjusting the saturation of the entire image with the Hue/Saturation adjustment. In this section we'll look primarily at the Hue setting. Adjusting the Hue setting of the entire image (the master setting) can produce some strange and amazing results. You're more likely to sample colour from the image to focus the adjustment on a limited range of colours instead. You can target and individually adjust reds, yellows, greens, cyans, blues and magentas.

The two coloured bands at the bottom of the dialogue represent how the adjustment will transform colours. The top band represents the original colours in the image, while the bottom band moves to show what each colour will be translated to. When you sample a colour, marks between the two bands indicate the colours that have been targeted. Once you've specified a range of colours to work with, you can replace one hue with another and adjust the saturation of the selected colours as well.

1 Select Hue/Saturation from the black and white circle menu at the bottom of the Layers panel to add the new layer.

2 Click the finger icon in the upper left corner of the Adjustments panel to activate the targeted adjustment pointer.

3 Press down the mouse button on a colour in the image that you would like to change and keep holding the button down. The Adjustments panel will update, showing the colours you have targeted.

4 Drag to the right to increase saturation or to the left to decrease saturation. Release the mouse button when you have a satisfactory result.

5 Move the Hue slider to locate a colour that makes the image look more interesting. Re-adjust the saturation as required after selecting a new hue.

6 You can also move the handles on the colour display at the bottom to adjust the colour mapping. The inner handles represent colours that will be converted 100%. The outer handles determine what colours are partially affected. Sometimes it helps to move the Hue slider all the way to the left to visualise where the changes are happening as you adjust the handles and then move the hue back to your intended position.

7 Optional: select another colour group via the menu or use the targeting tool to click in the image and adjust more colours.

8 Optional: paint black into the layer mask where you don't want the effect to apply.

> ▶ **SEE ALSO:** You can produce a different colourisation effect using the Hue/Saturation adjustment with the Colorize option turned on. You can't target colours through the dialogue when the option is active, but you can use the Color Range command and build a mask to selectively colourise areas of the image. You can also use the Hue/Saturation adjustment to colourise black and white images, which we'll cover later in this chapter. See Chapters 11 and 12 for details on making selections and masks.

Adjust colour with RGB channels

You can adjust individual colour channels in the Curves adjustment to remove colour casts or intentionally colourise an image. The colour channels in the Curves adjustment work on the basis of three principles of additive colour: a) mixtures of the three spectral primaries (red, green and blue) produce all other colours; b) equal amounts of red, green and blue combine to produce a neutral grey, black or white; c) each of the primaries has a complement (an opposing colour) that neutralises it to produce grey.

Each colour channel in the Curves adjustment controls the mixture of a pair of opposing colours as follows: Red/Cyan, Green/Magenta,Blue/Yellow. So, if an image looks as though it has too much cyan in it, you can compensate by pushing the red channel curve towards red.

When the adjustment layer is in the Normal blending mode, adding red, green or blue to the curve will lighten the image and pushing the curve towards cyan, magenta or yellow will darken it. You can prevent the curve from affecting tonality by changing its blending mode to Color. In general, you can add a point near the middle of the curve and push up or down in a diagonal direction to apply the adjustment.

1 Add a Curves adjustment layer and rename it to indicate that it's a colour adjustment curve.

2 Set the blending mode of the layer to Color.

3 Select a channel from the menu immediately above the graph area.

4 Click on the line to add a point and drag to adjust. Moving the middle tones has the most pronounced effect.

5 Work one channel at a time and toggle the adjustment layer on and off with the eyeball icon to evaluate the results.

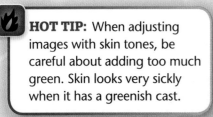

HOT TIP: When adjusting images with skin tones, be careful about adding too much green. Skin looks very sickly when it has a greenish cast.

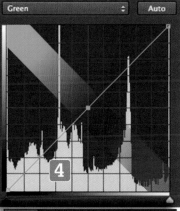

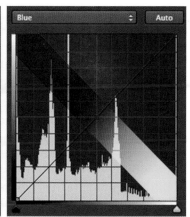

Use a colour lookup adjustment

Colour lookup layers are an exciting new feature in Photoshop CS6 that allow you to apply colour lookup tables (also known as LUTs) to your images. They work by transforming the RGB numbers in your image to produce often dramatically different looks with just a couple of clicks. A number of colour lookups are installed, and you can also load others from your hard drive.

The technology for these adjustments has been used for some time in the film industry, originally to match the look of film or video from different sources. Now LUTs are used for creative aesthetic effects as well. Photoshop's Colour Lookup layers work with three different types of colour lookups: 3DLUTs, Abstract Profiles and Device Links.

1 Select Color Lookup from the menu at the bottom of the Layers panel to add a new layer or double-click the thumbnail of a Color Lookup layer to show its controls in the Properties panel.

2 To apply a colour lookup, in the Properties panel, select an item from one of the three menus.

3 To compare before and after, click the eyeball icon at the bottom of the panel to toggle the effect.

4 To select a colour lookup from your hard drive, select Load [colour lookup type] from a menu.

5 Clicking the radio button (circle) on the left side of the panel activates the menu item associated with it. If it is a colour lookup, that effect will be applied. If the item reads Load [colour lookup type], the file open dialogue will appear, as in the previous step.

HOT TIP: There are many ways to create a sepia-tone image in Photoshop, but the Sepia abstract profile may produce the best results yet. The Gray Tone abstract profile is a convenient and simple way to convert images to black and white, and it produces a better result than setting the saturation to –100 in a Hue/Saturation layer.

Use Black & White adjustment

The Black & White adjustment layer is an extremely effective and flexible means of converting colour images into neutral black and white. Compared with the many other methods available in Photoshop to produce black and white images, it gives you the most direct control over the quality of the translation of colours into greyscale tones. The adjustment mimics what black and white film does by converting reds, yellows, greens, cyans, blues and magentas into distinct shades of grey. (Film's sensitivity to light varies by wavelength, so different colours are rendered in different shades of grey.) The Photoshop adjustment goes one better by enabling you to alter the shades of grey that correspond to each colour.

In the Layers panel, select the top layer and then select Black & White from the New Adjustment Layer icon at the bottom of the panel. You can click the Auto button or choose a pre-set from the menu at the top of the Properties panel to start. You can use the methods below to start from scratch or to tweak the results of your initial settings.

1 Click the finger icon in the panel, then drag right or left in the image to automatically select the corresponding sliders and lighten or darken tones.

2 You can manually adjust the sliders one at a time to find the right tonal mix.

3 Toggle the effect with the eyeball icon at the bottom of the panel to check your results as required.

4 Optional: once you have the desired tonal mix, add adjustments to the Layers panel (e.g. Curves) to refine contrast, open shadows, etc.

5 Optional: blacken parts of the mask on the Black & White layer to show isolated elements in colour. The quality of the masking will depend upon the precision of your painting. You can paint freehand or use selection and masking tools to make more exact masks.

6 Optional: reduce the opacity of the Black & White layer to allow some colour through.

7 Optional: change the blending mode of the Black & White layer to Luminosity. The resulting image will use the colours from the underlying layers but the tonality of the Black & White layer.

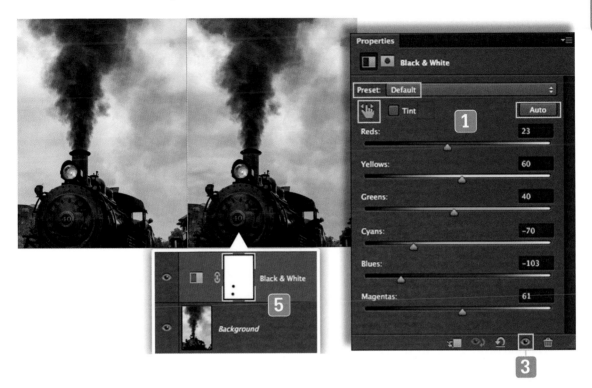

▶ **SEE ALSO:** We'll look at colourising a black and white image later in this chapter. Selections and masks will be covered in the next two chapters.

Use a gradient map adjustment

Gradient Maps assign colours to your image based on tonality (light and dark values), so you can use them with colour or black and white images. They can produce an extraordinary array of effects, from dramatic colourisation to simulated platinum and selenium-toned darkroom prints. To add a Gradient Map adjustment, select Gradient Map from the New Adjustment Layer menu at the bottom of the Layers panel. The mapping controls will appear in the Properties panel.

1 In the Properties panel, click the button at the right edge of the gradient to open the picker.

2 Use the gear icon menu in the picker to manage its content:

- You can change the way gradients appear in the picker (i.e. text, thumbnails or lists).
- To load additional gradient libraries (e.g. Photographic Toning), select a library and then either append or replace the current list of gradients.

3 Click in the display area of the picker to select a gradient (e.g. spectrum).

4 Once a gradient is selected, you can refine the appearance of your image by editing the gradient. Click on the gradient to open the Gradient Editor. A preset picker (that works like the gradient picker discussed above) appears in the top portion of the dialogue.

5 The markers along the bottom of the gradient are colour stops and the markers along the top are opacity stops. Click above or below the gradient to add new stops.

6 Click on the stops and use the controls at the bottom of the dialogue to adjust them. You can also drag to reposition them. To remove a stop, drag it away from the gradient until it snaps off.

7 Click the colour swatch or double-click on a colour stop to use the Color Picker.

8 Click OK to apply the edits to your gradient and close the Gradient Editor.

Colourise a black and white image

Adding monochromatic colour back to a black and white image can give it a more artistic interpretation. Certain colours (such as sepia) can immediately make a photo look more 'retro', while others can add emotional impact. The Hue/Saturation and Photo Filter adjustments offer different sets of options for colourising black and white images. Both can create sepia-tone images, but the default Photo filter is a much more subtle effect. The Photo Filter offers more pre-set colour options and uses the Color Picker, allowing you to specify colour selections more precisely than you can with the Hue/Saturation dialogue. Either of these effects can also be localised – applied to selected areas within the image – with the use of a layer mask. You can also 'hand-tint' your images, as many photographers did in the darkroom, by painting into a layer on top.

1 Add a Hue/Saturation adjustment: select Hue/Saturation from the New Adjustment Layer icon at the bottom of the Layers panel.

- Select the Sepia or Cyanotype pre-set to automatically activate the Colorize option and set default Hue and Saturation values.

  Or:

- Tick the Colorize option in the Properties panel and use the Hue slider to alter the colour.

- Optional: adjust the Saturation setting for either of the above methods to tune the effect.

2 Add a Photo Filter adjustment layer: select Photo Filter from the New Adjustment Layer icon.

- Click the radio button (circle) next to Filter and select a colour (e.g. Deep Emerald) from the menu or click on the colour chip to select a colour via the Color Picker.

 HOT TIP: The Photo Filter adjustment is great for use with colour images, too, especially the warming and cooling filters.

- Adjust density as required.
- Make sure you toggle the box marked Preserve Luminosity and evaluate its effect.
- You can also experiment with the blending mode of the Photo Filter layer.

3 Add a hand-tint layer: select the topmost layer and click the New Layer icon at the bottom of the Layers panel to add a blank layer. Select a starting blending mode such as Color.

- Activate the Brush tool (tap the B key) and set the foreground colour.
- Paint in the tinting layer as you like. You can paint with reduced opacity, different colours or brushes.
- Optional: adjust the blending mode to alter the effect of the painting.

4 Optional additional adjustments:

- Reduce the opacity of the colourising layer to moderate its effect.
- Change the Blend If settings of your colourising layers to refine their interaction with the layers beneath.
- Add a Curves layer to adjust tones on top of the Photo Filter.
- Tweak colour with Hue/Saturation or Vibrance.

Clip an adjustment to another layer

Clipping masks define themselves by the content of the 'base' layer. When you clip an adjustment layer to another layer, the adjustment applies only to the visible parts of the layer it is clipped to. That makes clipping masks very handy in compositing, because it allows you to attach colour adjustments to individual bits of your composition and match them to the rest. You can clip multiple layers of different types together. In the example, a colour inversion layer affects both Layers 1 and 2 until the adjustment is clipped to Layer 2. The balloon on the left shows the appearance of the composition before and after the adjustment has been added.

1   Position the cursor over the border between two layers you want to clip together.

2   Hold down the Option | Alt key (the cursor will change to the clipping icon) and click on the line.

3   The layers will clip together. The clipped layer indents and shows a bent arrow icon. The layer underneath becomes the base.

4   To unclip layers, Option | Alt-click on the line. The cursor will change shape to indicate that you are about to release the clipping mask.

▶ **SEE ALSO:** In Chapter 14, we'll use text as a base layer and clip an image to it.

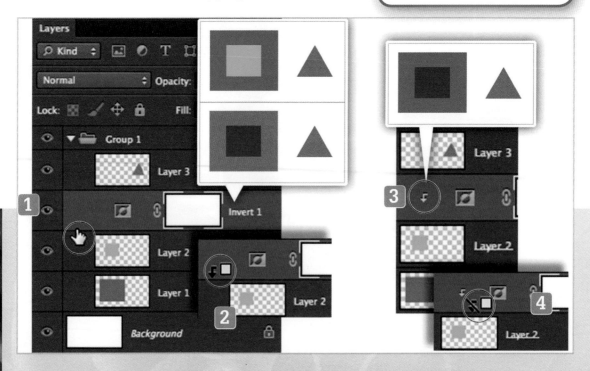

Use HDR Toning

HDR Toning can create the popular look of High Dynamic Range (HDR) images without the multi-exposure process needed to create true HDR images, but its real strength lies in the fact that you can edit tones with finesse in a massive 32-bit space. The command needs to flatten your layers to work, but you can restore your layers after toning and integrate the HDR version with the original.

1 Click on the Background layer and select Image, Adjustments, HDR Toning from the menu bar. If you get a message confirming that you want to flatten the image, click Yes. The HDR Toning dialogue will open.

2 Select a pre-set or toning method from one of the two menus at the top of the dialogue.

3 Adjust relevant controls (only the Exposure and Gamma and Local Adaptation methods have controls).

4 Toggle the preview tick box as you work to evaluate your results.

5 To use the toning curve, if you've used curves in Photoshop, shadows, midtones and highlights are not where you would expect them to be. Click in the image to show a bubble indicating where that tone sits on the curve.

- To place a point on the graph: Command | Control-click in the image or click on the graph.
- To adjust points: click on points to select. Use the arrow keys or drag the points to adjust.

6 Optional: save a pre-set via the icon next to the Preset menu.

7 Click OK to apply the adjustment. (Your adjusted version is likely to look better than the preview you saw.)

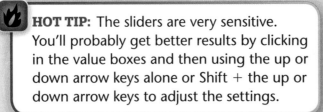

HOT TIP: The sliders are very sensitive. You'll probably get better results by clicking in the value boxes and then using the up or down arrow keys alone or Shift + the up or down arrow keys to adjust the settings.

8 To restore your layers:

- Activate the History panel and click the History Brush Source box on the left edge of the HDR Toning history state. An icon will appear in the box.

- Click the label of the history state immediately above the Flatten Image state. Your layers will return and the HDR-adjusted version will disappear.

- In the Layers panel, select the topmost layer and click the New Layer button to create an empty layer. Rename it HDR, if you like.

- To restore your HDR adjustment as a layer, select Edit, Fill from the menu bar and then select History from the Use menu in the dialogue that appears. Click OK.

9 Optional: integrate your HDR adjustment with the original version of the image by applying any of these techniques to the HDR layer:

- Try Luminosity, Soft Light or another blending mode.

- Adjust its opacity as needed.

- Add a mask to apply the HDR layer selectively.

11 Work with selections

Introduction

Selections are an essential tool for harnessing Photoshop's power. Just as you select a layer before performing an operation upon it, you can select regions of the image to modify or duplicate. Selections can be used to constrain painting, filling and deleting, and they can also be used as the basis for creating masks.

Selections can be simple geometric shapes, or based upon tones or colours in your image. Pixels can be partially selected to produce soft-edged effects. Selections can also be combined and modified in many ways, and they can be translated into masks and alpha channels, which can in turn be translated back into selections.

In the same way that you use a screwdriver and a saw for different tasks, Photoshop offers a range of tools for making different types of selections. Some will finish the job at hand a lot faster than others.

Use the Marquee tools

The Marquee tools are the most rudimentary of the selection tools, but you are likely to use them again and again. Simply hold down the mouse button and drag to create a 'marching ants' outline. You can easily switch between the rectangular and elliptical Marquee tools with a keystroke.

1 To activate the Marquee tool, tap M, use Shift + M to rotate through the tools, or select a Marquee tool from the fly-out menu.

2 Drag diagonally in any direction to create the selection. As you drag, a heads-up display tells you the size of your selection. To change the units of the display, adjust the rulers' scale setting (see composition aids in Chapter 8).

3 Hold down the Shift key as you drag to make perfect squares or circles.

4 Hold the Option | Alt key and drag to centre the selection around a point.

5 You can combine Shift and Option | Alt to centre circular or square selections.

6 'Marching ants' appear when you release the mouse button to show the resulting selection.

7 Command | Ctrl + A performs the Select, All command, which draws a rectangular marquee around the edge of your image.

8 If you don't like the selection you've created, you can use Command | Ctrl + D (Select, Deselect from the menu) to clear the selection and start again.

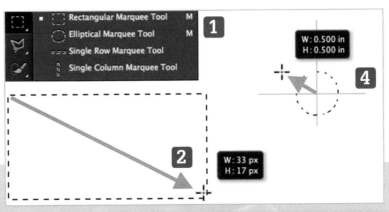

HOT TIP: The cursor for the Marquee tool is very small. If you lose sight of it, hold down the space bar to show the Hand Tool cursor. Wiggle the mouse if you need to. Once you find your mouse pointer, you can position it where you need it and then release the space bar to return to the Marquee tool.

Use Lasso tools

The Lasso is a free-form selection tool that is best for loose, irregular selections. In this section, we will look at the Free Form and Polygonal Lassos. You draw an outline with either tool, then Photoshop displays 'marching ants' to indicate an active selection.

1 Tap L to activate the current Lasso, use Shift + L to cycle through the Lasso tools, or use the menu in the Tools panel to select either the Lasso tool or the Polygonal Lasso.

2 You'll usually want to use this tool in the New Selection mode (shown selected here), but you can use a different mode as required.

3 Optional: set a Feather value in the Options panel. If you're not sure what value to use, set it to zero. You can always feather the selection after it has been created.

4 Make sure that the box marked Anti-alias is ticked.

5 With the Lasso: drag out a shape with the Lasso. Release the mouse button at any time to close the path.

6 With the Polygonal Lasso: click to place angle points. The tool will connect the points to create your selection. Hold down the Shift key to force the tool to draw horizontal, vertical and 45-degree lines. Double-click anywhere or click on the starting point to close the selection.

7 Optional: hold down the Option | Alt key to convert the Lasso into the Polygonal Lasso or vice versa on the fly. Release the key to revert to the tool you began with. This allows you to combine free-form and polygonal selection shapes.

8 Optional: if your shape starts to get out of hand, as you're drawing hit the Esc key to cancel what you have done so far.

9 If you don't like the selection you've created, you can use Command | Ctrl + D (Select, Deselect from the menu) to clear the selection and start again.

ALERT: It's generally best to use the Anti-alias option with any of the selection tools that offer it, including the Lasso and the Elliptical Marquee tools. You cannot add anti-aliasing after you have created the selection.

 SEE ALSO: Modify a selection, deselect and reselect later in this chapter for more on selection modes.

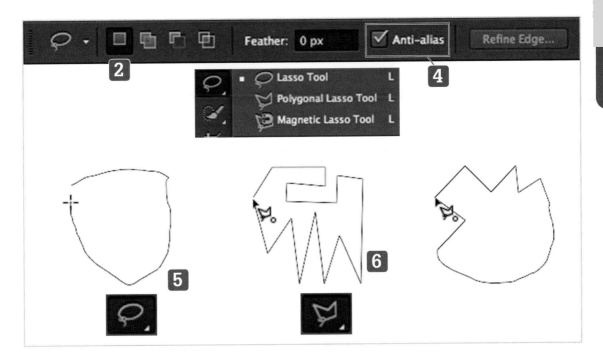

Reposition a selection

You can move any selection by activating the Marquee tool (tap M) and dragging or using the arrow keys. It doesn't matter what tool was used to create the selection; all selections behave in the same manner once they're created.

1 When you position the Marquee tool's mouse pointer over an active selection, its icon will change to show that the selection can be repositioned.

2 Tap the arrow keys to nudge the selection one pixel at a time.

3 Hold down the Shift key and tap the arrow keys to bump the selection 10 pixels at a time.

! **ALERT:** The Move tool will drag the selected pixels along with the selection.

Visualise selections with Quick Mask

The Quick Mask mode allows you to view selections as a coloured overlay instead of marching ants. It's being covered early in this chapter because we'll use it to illustrate a number of techniques along the way. Later in this chapter, we'll cover some other Quick Mask applications. The default Quick Mask settings display a translucent red overlay that isn't always easy to read. We'll change the setting to make the Quick Mask show the selected areas as a bright green silhouette.

1 In the Tools panel, double-click on the Quick Mask icon to open the Quick Mask Options dialogue.

2 Set Color Indicates to Selected Areas.

3 In the Color section, change the opacity to 100% and click on the colour chip to display the Color Picker dialogue.

4 Select a colour such as fluorescent green (e.g. #66ff00), which is likely to stand out clearly against almost any image that you can possibly edit. Click OK to accept your colour choice.

5 Click OK to accept the Quick Mask options.

6 Note that the Quick Mask icon is darkened, the document title contains the words 'Quick Mask' and the active layer is highlighted in grey. These indicate that you are in Quick Mask mode.

7 Tap the Q key to exit Quick Mask mode.

8 To test your settings, make a selection with the Marquee tool and then tap Q to see the Quick Mask. Tap Q a second time to exit Quick Mask.

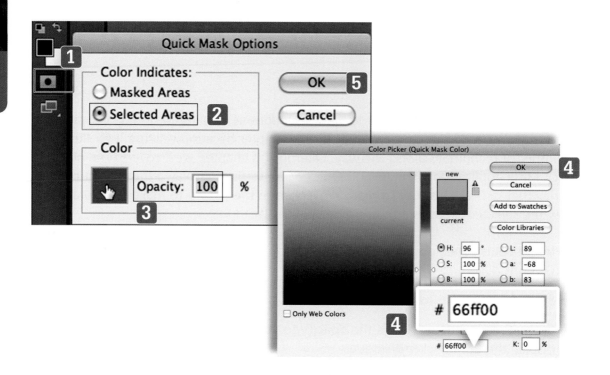

 HOT TIP: With the settings we have just made, the bright green, opaque mask will completely cover the selected areas. There may be times when you'll need to see details in the selected area. When that happens, you can reopen the Quick Mask Options dialogue and reduce the opacity.

Use the Quick Selection tool

While many people refer to the Magic Wand as the 'Tragic Wand', its sibling, the Quick Selection tool, lives up to its name and largely does what people expected the Magic Wand to do: you simply 'paint' over areas of your image to intelligently select them. It does a much better job at finding edges and completely selecting areas without leaving the little holes that the Magic Wand is known for. Of course, it works best when the areas that you want to select have well-defined edges, meaning strong tonal or colour contrast. If the edges are less well defined, the tool can grab an area that you don't want. When that happens, you can switch to Subtract mode and clear the unwanted part of the selection. Even though it's not perfect, it can often get you a good rough selection faster than other tools. You can then refine that selection with other tools, such as the Refine Edge command.

1 Hold down the mouse button and select the Quick Selection tool from the Tools panel or tap W or Shift + W to cycle from the Magic Wand.

2 Optional: tick Sample All Layers in the Options bar to make a selection based on all layers in the image, instead of the currently selected layer.

3 Optional: tick Auto-Enhance to reduce roughness and blockiness in the selection boundary.

4 Adjust the brush size: tap the [and] (square bracket) keys, or hold down Ctrl + Option (Windows: Alt + Right-click) and drag left or right.

5 Paint over the areas you want to select.

6 Hold down the Option | Alt key and drag the mouse over areas you want to deselect.

7 Optional: tap the Q key to toggle Quick Mask and see your selection as an overlay instead of marching ants.

8 The default selection mode is Add to Selection, so if you release the mouse button and start painting again, the tool will select additional areas. You can also change the mode to start a new selection each time you start to paint or to subtract from the selection without holding the Option | Alt key.

SEE ALSO: Once any area in your image is selected, the Refine Edge button becomes available. See the section on using the Refine Mask dialogue in Chapter 12.

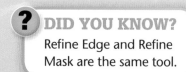

? DID YOU KNOW?
Refine Edge and Refine Mask are the same tool.

Select by colour range

Did you ever want to select just the sky in a photo, or everything that wasn't the sky? Or perhaps you want to select someone by finding the skin tones in your image. This is the tool to do just that. You can also use it to select highlights, midtones, shadows or specific colours. The selections you'll make with this tool are perfect precursors for masks.

1 Click on the topmost layer and choose Select, Color Range from the menu bar to open the dialogue and use the Select menu to determine how to find colours.

2 Choose Sampled Colors from the menu to select by clicking in the image.
- Start with a Fuzziness of approximately 30.
- Click to set the first sample and then Shift-click or Shift-drag across a small area to select additional colours. You can click in the main image window or in the dialogue.

3 Optional: tick Localized Color Clusters to focus your selection around the area you're clicking in. Use the Range slider to control the focus.

4 If unwanted areas start to become selected, use Command | Ctrl + Z to undo and try sampling elsewhere. You can also Option | Alt-click to subtract colours. (The + and – droppers do the same thing as Shift-clicking or Option | Alt-clicking.)

5 Choose Skin Tones from the menu to select colours related to skin. You can tick Detect Faces to do a better job of selecting people when their eyes are visible.

6 Refine your selection by adjusting the Fuzziness control. Increasing the setting selects more colours and usually softens the edges of the selection. (It's generally best to keep the Fuzziness relatively low and take more colour samples. Setting the Fuzziness too high can select areas you don't want and setting it too low can result in a jagged selection.)

7 The Color Range dialogue defaults to showing the image in its display area. Hold down the Command | Ctrl key to temporarily display the selection, or click on Selection to change the display.

8 Use the Selection Preview menu to see your selection in the main image window. The Quick Mask option uses the preferences discussed recently and the Grayscale option shows what the selection would look like as a mask.

9 Ticking the Invert box in the dialogue does the same thing as choosing Select, Inverse from the menu bar after you OK the dialogue.

10 Click OK to create the selection. Photoshop will display marching ants to indicate that something is selected.

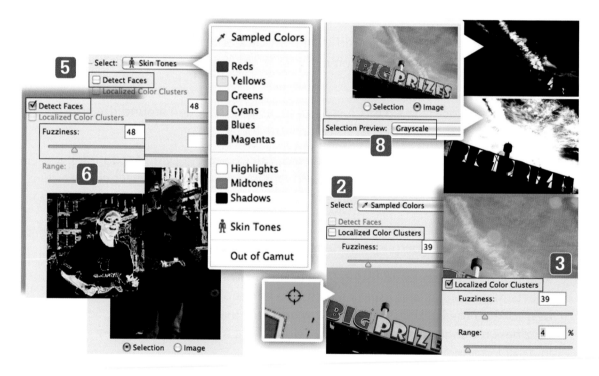

 HOT TIP:

- Instead of using the Localized Color Clusters option, you can select part of your image before opening the Color Range dialogue. The colour range selection will apply only to the initially selected area.

- The Skin Tones option is smart enough to recognise skin colours from a broad range of ethnicities.

Modify a selection, deselect and reselect

The selection tools have their limits, and sometimes you can't select what you want in one go. Starting from a rough selection, you can refine it to build up a complex selection, combining different tools and adding or subtracting simple selections, step by step. At other times, it's easier to select what you don't want and invert the selection. You can tap Q at any time to check your progress with Quick Mask. Many selection tools produce very hard edges, which you can soften with feathering. For those times when it makes sense to start again from scratch or you no longer need a selection, you can discard a selection with a keystroke that is worth memorising.

1. Using the Marquee, Lasso and Quick Select tools, you can make an initial selection, then make additional selections with any other tool using the following modes. You can change the mode in the Options bar or hold down the indicated modifier keys as you make additional selections:

   - Use Add to Selection (Shift) to combine the selections.
   - Use Subtract From Selection (Option | Alt) to remove areas.
   - Use Intersect With Selection (Shift + Option | Alt) to select the region that both selections have in common.

2. To localise the Color Range command, make a selection and then choose Select, Color Range from the menu bar. The resulting selection will be confined to the region of the first selection (an intersection selection).

3. Several techniques for modifying selections (marching ants) include the following:

   - Go to Select, Modify in the menu bar to reveal a submenu or Control-click | Right-click in the selection to reveal a menu with options that include Select Inverse, Feather and Refine Edge.

ALERT: There is a very different but similar-sounding command that inverts pixels: Image, Adjustments, Invert (Command | Ctrl + I). If you accidentally choose that command, just use Command | Ctrl + Z to undo.

- Choose Select, Transform Selection from the menu bar to display transformation handles for the selection. Drag the handles to free transform the selection or Control-click | Right-click inside the handles to display a menu and select a transformation mode.

4 You can also click Refine Edge in the Options bar. The dialogue allows you to smooth, feather and shift the edges of your selection. The Contrast slider controls how gradually the feathering falls off. The dialogue shows a preview as you adjust your selection. Tap F to cycle through and select a view mode (e.g. Overlay is Quick Mask). Each view mode has its own keyboard shortcut as well.

5 The menu command Select, Inverse (Shift + Command | Ctrl + I) inverts a selection: what was previously unselected becomes selected, and what was previously selected is deselected.

6 To discard a selection, choose Select, Deselect (Command | Ctrl + D) from the menu bar.

7 To restore the last selection, use Select, Reselect (Shift + Command | Ctrl + D).

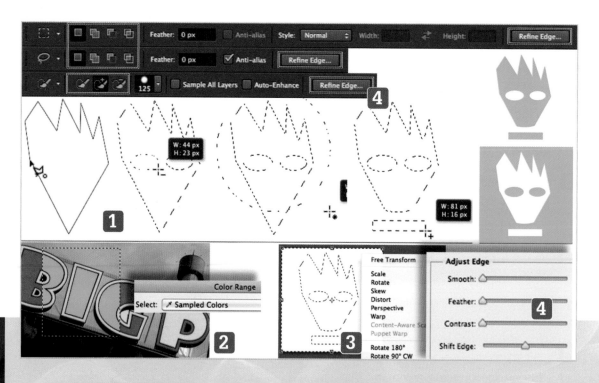

SEE ALSO: Refine Edge and Refine Mask are the same command. We'll cover edge detection in Chapter 12.

Modify or create a selection with Quick Mask

You can use the Quick Mask tool to paint a selection by eye, either modifying to an existing selection or starting a new one. There is a slight twist to seeing how your mask is fitting: you can temporarily invert the mask and look for gaps. You can also change your Quick Mask preferences to make the Quick Mask overlay translucent. The example shows a selection that's been started with the Polygonal Lasso tool. We'll look at how you can fill in the curved part using Quick Mask with a 50% hardness brush.

1 Tap the Q key to enter Quick Mask mode.

2 Tap the D key to set default colours: black foreground, white background.

3 Paint with black to colour-in areas. Paint with white to remove coloured areas from the mask. (Tap X to swap foreground and background colours.)

4 Vary the brush size and hardness as required to paint with black over the part of the image that you want to select. You can also paint at lower opacity and flow to build up coverage. Don't worry if you overshoot.

5 To see whether you have over-painted any edges, hit Command | Ctrl + I (Menu: Image, Adjustments, Invert) to invert the mask.

6 To make the overlay translucent, double-click the Quick Mask button in the Tools panel to reveal the Quick Mask preferences dialogue, reduce the opacity, then click OK. Opening the dialogue toggles Quick Mask, so you'll need to tap Q to toggle it again.

7 If you inverted the mask in step 5, invert the mask again with Command | Ctrl + I, or your selection will be inverted when you exit Quick Mask.

8 When your quick mask is complete, tap the Q key to exit and note the marching ants.

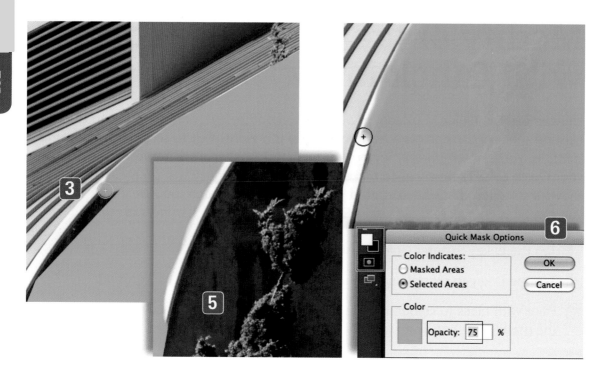

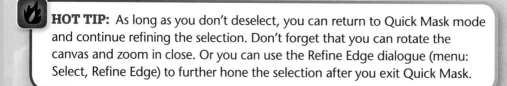

Load and save selections

Photoshop offers a number of ways to convert elements of your image into useful selections. You can enhance those selections with techniques from this chapter. Once you've spent more than a minute or two creating a selection, you might also appreciate being able to save and re-use them. When you save a selection, it is normally stored as an alpha channel, which appears in the Channels panel. You can also save selections into layer masks. You use the same keystroke to load selections from alpha channels, masks and layer thumbnails.

1 To open the Save Selection dialogue, choose Select, Save Selection from the menu bar. If the Marquee tool is active, you can also Control-click | Right-click inside the selection and select Save Selection from the menu that appears.

2 To save a selection as a new alpha channel, set the Channel menu to New, enter a name and click OK.

3 To save a selection to a layer mask, you'll need to select a layer with a mask before opening the Save Selection dialogue:

- Select the layer's mask from the Channel menu.
- The default operation is to replace the existing mask. You can also modify the mask by performing add, subtract or intersect operations.

4 When two or more open documents have the same dimensions, you can save selections between them. Select an item from the document menu. If you do not enter a name, Photoshop will assign one for you.

5 To load a layer's opacity as a selection, Command | Control-click on its thumbnail. The mouse pointer changes shape to indicate that the selection will be loaded.

6 To load a layer mask as a selection, Command | Control-click on its thumbnail.

 HOT TIP: Many masks contain gradients. When you load them as a selection, the marching ants indicate where the density of the mask reaches at least 50%.

7 To load a saved selection, choose Select, Load Selection from the menu bar. The Load Selection dialogue will appear:

- Select a channel from the menu.
- Choose an operation (New, Add, Subtract or Intersect).
- Optional: to select the inverse of the selection you're loading, tick the box marked Invert.
- Click OK.

8 To load a channel as a selection, open the Channels panel and Command | Control-click on any thumbnail.

- Loading a saved selection through the Channels panel is the same as using the Load Selection dialogue.
- Load the RGB channel to select the brightest parts of the image. Choose Select, Inverse afterwards to select the darkest parts of the image instead. (The results are different from selecting highlights or shadows with the Select, Color Range command.) These can be very useful selections to make as precursors for adding Curves.

Use selections

This section will provide an overview of ways to use selections. Some of these capabilities have already been discussed or hinted at in earlier sections, but they are worthy of repeating here. Selections work like masking tape in the physical world: the deselected areas will be protected and only the selected areas will receive the colour or the effect. If you create a selection before adding an adjustment layer or adding a layer mask, the selection will automatically be converted to a mask for the new layer and the effect will be constrained by the mask in the same way that the selection constrains painting. When a selection is feathered, effects will be applied partially across the feathered area, and the marching ants will surround areas where the pixels are at least 50% selected. The moving pattern of the marching ants can be distracting, so there is a way to hide it.

1 Optional: use Command | Ctrl + H (menu: View, Extras) to hide or show Extras, including the marching ants. (On the Mac, you may be asked whether you want the keystroke to hide extras or hide the application.)

2 Paint (or apply the Eraser tool) on the layer as you normally would. Changes 'stick' only to the areas that are selected. Partially selected areas will receive translucent changes.

3 Select Edit, Fill from the menu bar to use the Fill dialogue. Choose one of the preset colours or select Color from the Use menu to open the Color Picker.

4 Use Option + Delete | Alt + Backspace to fill the selection with the foreground colour from the Tools panel.

5 Use Command + Delete | Ctrl + Backspace to fill the selection with the background colour.

6 Select Edit, Stroke from the menu bar to outline the selection. To centre your stroke over the selection border, enter an odd number for the Width. Click the Color swatch to open the Color Picker.

7 To convert a selection to a layer mask, do any of the following:

- Click the Add layer mask icon at the bottom of the Layers panel.
- Use the menu at the bottom of the Layers panel to add a new fill or adjustment layer.
- See the previous section for details on saving a selection to a layer mask.

8 Use Command | Ctrl + J to copy the selected pixels to a new layer. Shift + Command | Ctrl + J cuts the pixels out of the selected layer and moves them to a new layer.

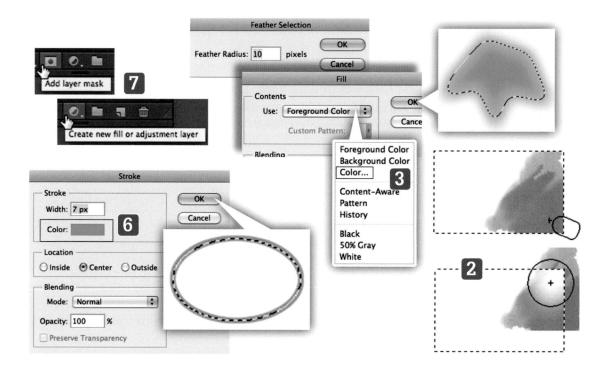

SEE ALSO: As we saw in Chapters 6 and 7, you can use selections to erase parts of a layer, to move pixels within a layer, and to copy or cut pixels out of a layer and place them into a new layer. One of the options in the Fill dialogue, Content-Aware Fill, will be discussed in Chapter 13. Remember, there are lots of ways to set the foreground colour before you fill. See Chapter 9.

12 Work with masks

Introduction

Layer masks are a core element of a non-destructive editing strategy. Instead of permanently erasing pixels, you can mask a layer and render the pixels invisible. If you discover later that you have removed too much or too little, you can simply edit the mask. You can use masks with any object you can add to the Layers panel, and several types automatically include a neutral mask when you create them.

Masks are made up of pixels, each one corresponding to a pixel in the layer that the mask is attached to. The tonal values of the mask's pixels determine the visibility of the pixels in the layer as follows: black pixels in the mask have a value of zero and hide the corresponding layer pixels. White pixels have a value of 255, and fully reveal the corresponding pixels. Thus, an all-white mask is neutral – it has no effect on its layer – while an all-black mask renders the layer invisible. As the grey value of pixels in the mask increases (the pixels get lighter), they reveal progressively more of the layer, making it possible to feather and blend images and adjustments.

We'll look more closely at these topics in the rest of this chapter.

Use layer masks

Layer masks operate on the principle that 'black blocks', rendering pixels, adjustments or effects invisible. An all-black mask makes its layer invisible, while an all-white mask behaves the same as no mask at all. Adjustment layers, Fill layers, and Smart Filters all include a white (neutral) layer mask when you create them. While the effect of the mask can be obvious, you usually don't see the mask itself, but work with the mask indirectly. A thumbnail in the Layers panel gives some indication of the shape of the mask at all times, and you can reveal the mask on the canvas (the image editing area) in several ways when you need to.

1. To begin editing a mask, click on its thumbnail in the Layers panel. Marks will appear around the corners of the thumbnail to indicate that the mask is selected for editing.

2. To localise adjustments such as a contrast curve or hue/saturation adjustment, you can adjust the entire image first and then use Command | Ctrl + I to invert the all-white mask (which turns it black). You can then paint with a white brush over the areas where you want to apply the effect.

3. When painting a mask, you can use reduced opacity or flow to gradually shade it. In most cases, a soft (low hardness setting) round brush works best. If you make part of the mask too dark, switch to white and paint over the same area to reverse the effect. When you start to edit a mask, Photoshop defaults to white for the foreground and black for the background. Just tap X to swap colours.

4. You can add masks to layers and groups – just click to select it, then click on the Add layer mask icon at the bottom of the Layers panel.

5. You can fill a mask with a solid shade, paint in it, apply a gradient or even run filters on it.

6. If you make a selection before you add a layer mask or create a layer that includes one, Photoshop will convert the selection into the mask for that object. The black parts of the resulting mask will correspond to the parts of the layer that were not selected.

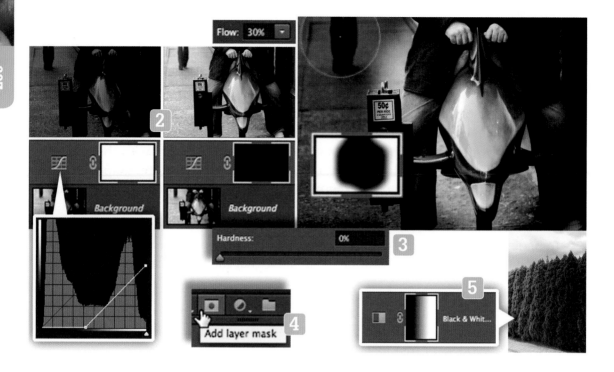

Flow: 30%

Background

Background

Hardness: 0%

Add layer mask

Black & Whit...

2 3 4 5

Adjust masks in the Properties panel

The Properties panel is new in Photoshop CS6. It includes several useful features for working with masks. The Density and Feather settings in the panel are non-destructive, i.e. you can change or revert those settings as many times as you like without degrading the mask. The example here was created by adding a Curves adjustment layer and then clicking the Color Range button in the Properties panel.

1 Double-click on the layer mask thumbnail to open the mask in the Properties panel.

2 Use the Density slider to make the mask lighter. This weakens any localisation by diluting dark pixels in the mask. Reducing the slider to zero turns the mask completely white.

3 Use the Feather slider to blur edges within the mask. This can help by blending hard transitions in your mask, but it can also create problematic haloes.

4 Click Mask Edge to open the Refine Mask dialogue. We'll look at this feature more closely in the next section.

5 Click Color Range to revise the mask by sampling colours within your image.

6 Click Invert to flip light and dark values and reverse what the mask shows or hides.

7 The buttons along the bottom of the panel from left to right perform the following functions:

- Load the mask as a selection. This is the same as Command | Control-clicking on the mask thumbnail.
- Click the Apply Mask button to recreate the effect of the mask by erasing pixels in the layer and discard the mask. Translucent pixels will be partially erased.

ALERT: Since applying a mask erases pixels, you might want to back up your work. For backup, you can duplicate the layer and make it invisible or use File, Save As to save a copy with the layer mask before applying the mask. Veteran users of Photoshop may have learned to apply Gaussian Blur to a mask to soften its edges, but Feather does the same thing non-destructively.

- Click the eyeball icon to toggle the effect of the mask (you can also Shift-click on the mask thumbnail). A red X appears through the mask thumbnail when it is disabled, and the layer will appear as though it has no mask.
- Click the bin icon to discard the mask. You may be asked if you want to apply the mask. If you click Yes, the result will be the same as clicking the Apply Mask button.

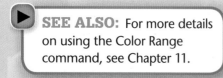

SEE ALSO: For more details on using the Color Range command, see Chapter 11.

Use the Refine Mask dialogue

This dialogue offers several tools to improve the edges in complex masks. The same dialogue comes up when you want to refine a selection prior to making it into a mask or saving it to an Alpha channel. The edge-detection tools in the dialogue are very powerful. The Smart Radius feature was designed for images that have a mix of hard and soft edges.

1. To open the dialogue, double-click the mask thumbnail in the Layers panel to display the mask in the Properties panel and then click the Mask Edge button. You can also click the mask to select it and choose Select, Refine Mask (Option + Command + R | Alt + Ctrl + R) from the menu bar.

2. Tap F to cycle through the view modes to find the one that works best for the image you are working on.

3. To use Edge Detection, move the Radius slider.

4. The Refine Radius brush is active by default. It is a brush that you can apply over problem areas to Paint with the tool (+ mode) to select elements, or hold down the Option | Alt key (– mode) to mask out elements. Use the square bracket keys to change the size of the brush.

5. Optional: tick the Smart Radius box and increase the radius for images that have a mix of hard and soft edges. To extract hair, the tool works especially well with very high radius settings.

6. Optional: toggle the Original (tap P) and the Radius (tap J) boxes in the View Mode section as required. *Note*: Radius can be slow to render.

7. Optional: use the Adjust Edge sliders. Smooth straightens jagged turns in the selection. Feather blurs the edge. Contrast makes the edge sharper, sometimes at the expense of fine detail. Shift Edge expands or contracts the selection area.

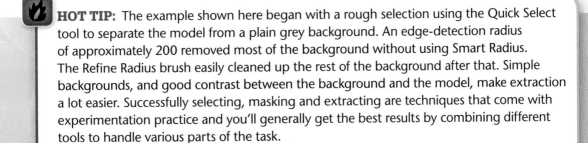

HOT TIP: The example shown here began with a rough selection using the Quick Select tool to separate the model from a plain grey background. An edge-detection radius of approximately 200 removed most of the background without using Smart Radius. The Refine Radius brush easily cleaned up the rest of the background after that. Simple backgrounds, and good contrast between the background and the model, make extraction a lot easier. Successfully selecting, masking and extracting are techniques that come with experimentation practice and you'll generally get the best results by combining different tools to handle various parts of the task.

8 If you have colour fringes, you can use the Output section to decontaminate them. Because the option alters colours, it always creates a new layer. To see how the colours are changing before you commit, tap the R key to activate the Reveal Layer view.

9 Click OK to apply the refinements.

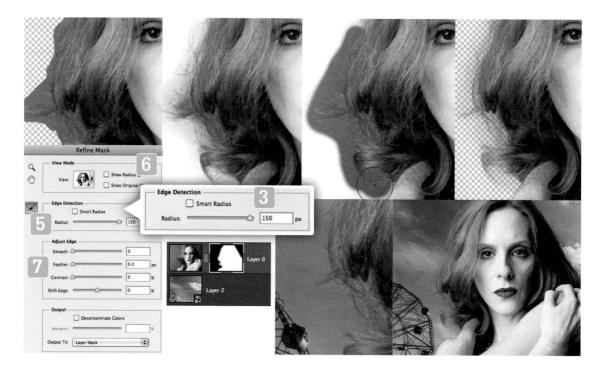

> **ALERT:** Since the Decontaminate Colors option creates a new layer, it is a good idea to keep the original (just make it invisible) so that you can revert to it if necessary.

Evaluate masking and view a mask as an overlay

One way to evaluate how well your mask is working is to temporarily disable it. Toggling the mask off and back on will demonstrate its effect. That's very helpful, but sometimes it's better to visualise a mask more directly. You can see the mask in context when you view it as an overlay that resembles Quick Mask mode. The overlay makes it easier to gauge whether a mask spills over an edge, or doesn't reach far enough, but Photoshop's default setting is to show masks as a 50% red overlay, which can be hard to read. You can change the Layer Mask Display Options to resemble the Quick Mask preferences used in Chapter 11.

1. To disable or enable a layer mask, hold down the Shift key and click on the layer mask. A red X will appear. You can also use the eyeball icon at the bottom of the mask controls in the Properties panel.

2. To toggle the mask overlay, click on the layer thumbnail to select it and then tap the \ (backslash) key.

3. When the thumbnail is selected, any painting you do will be applied to the mask and you'll see the overlay change.

4. To change the Layer Mask Display Options:
   - Control-click | Right-click on a layer mask and select Mask Options to open the settings dialogue.
   - Change the Opacity as required.
   - Click on the colour chip to open the Color Picker dialogue.
   - Select a colour that is not likely to appear in your image, e.g. fluorescent green (e.g. enter 66ff00 into the box marked # at the bottom of the dialogue).
   - Click OK to commit the Color Picker and then click OK to accept the setting.

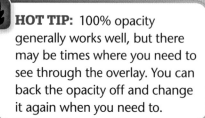

HOT TIP: 100% opacity generally works well, but there may be times where you need to see through the overlay. You can back the opacity off and change it again when you need to.

? DID YOU KNOW?

The 50% red default setting was not just a random value, it was designed to imitate the look of Rubylith – a masking material used in offset, gravure and screen-printing.

Work with a mask onscreen

Aside from viewing a mask as an overlay, you can bring the mask into the main image window to edit it directly.

1 Option | Alt-click on the mask thumbnail to view and modify the mask in the image editing area (the canvas) or return to the normal view.

2 You can make selections to constrain painting or use Edit, Fill to rapidly colour parts of your mask.

3 Paint in black or white to edit the mask. Use Opacity, Flow, Hardness and Brush Size to build tone slowly.

4 Optional: paint with the Color Dodge or Color Burn brush modes (these are the same as layer blending modes, but applied to the pixels as you paint) to solidify whites or blacks respectively:

- Set the brush opacity to 50% or less; set the opacity to approximately 30% if you want to be extra careful.
- A soft (zero % hardness) round brush generally works well.
- Set the foreground to white and the painting mode to Color Dodge to lighten. Only the greys lighter than 50% grey will be affected.
- Set the foreground to black and the painting mode to Color Burn to darken.
- Don't brush over the same area too many times or you'll lose the edge.

5 Another technique for editing masks is to paste a copy of the mask into itself, then fade with a blending mode:

- Select All: Use Command | Ctrl + A (Select, All from the menu bar).
- Copy the mask: use Command | Ctrl + C (Edit, Copy).
- Paste: Use Command | Ctrl + V (Edit, Paste).
- Fade to a blending mode: e.g. Color Dodge is excellent for brightening highlights and ignoring darks.

- Deselect: use Command | Ctrl + D (Select, Deselect).
- Optional: repeat, possibly with a different blending mode. It's important to deselect and select all again, or it won't work.

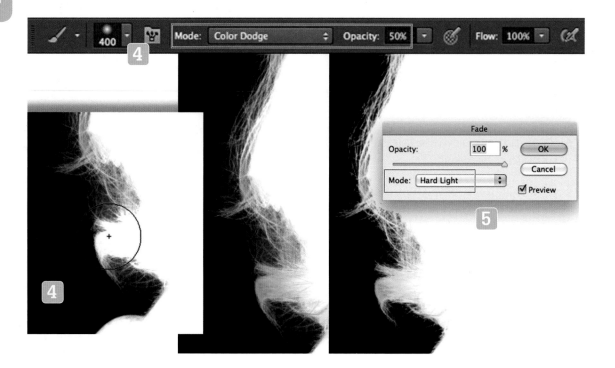

13 Retouch and manipulate

Introduction

Part of Photoshop's reputation is based on how artists can use it to create 'fake' imagery that is very believable. A common lament in some circles is that Photoshop makes such things 'too easy'. The truth is, it still takes vision and skill to make those illusions work, and even more skill to make them seem as though they're not illusions. The first step towards creating that kind of work is knowing that the tools exist and how to use them. In this chapter, we'll look at several ways of editing image content, including some of the fundamental tools and techniques for retouching. You can use these techniques along with layer techniques in Chapter 7 and colour and tone techniques in Chapter 10 to create sophisticated composite images. We'll scratch the surface here, but to use the techniques well requires experimentation and practice.

Here is a good set of practices for retouching and manipulating:

- Even if you're simply fixing a few blemishes in a portrait, make your edits in layers that can be revised or replaced later.
- Apply tools like the Healing Brush to a blank layer.
- Use smart objects when scaling layers or applying filters.
- Duplicate or stamp a layer to use with filters that can't be applied to smart objects or tools such as the Patch tool.

Of course, there will be occasional exceptions, but these practices will give you more options in the long run.

Use the Clone Stamp

The Clone Stamp is a brush tool that has the effect of copying and pasting (or transcribing) information from one part of your image to another. You load the Clone Stamp before you apply it by pointing at a location in the image to set a starting point to transcribe from. As you apply the brush, the location of the source tracks along with the brush and information is copied from the source location to the brush location. To aid in blending, you can clone at reduced opacity and flow, and you can feather the edge of the brush by reducing the hardness setting. You can clone into the same layer and alter the layer, or you can clone non-destructively into a blank layer with the Sample All Layers option.

You'll need to watch for differences in tone. Cloning from too light a source or too dark a source makes your work very obvious. Remember that you can step back in history to undo any problem cloning. If you're using a graphics tablet, check the Brush panel: if Shape Dynamics is turned on, you will have to press firmly to get the brush to match the size of the preview.

1 To prepare a layer to clone into, create a new blank layer, stamp a layer or duplicate a layer that you intend to retouch into. Click the layer to select it.

2 Tap S to activate the Clone Stamp tool. Make sure you've selected the Clone Stamp and not the Pattern Stamp, which is under the same button.

3 In the Options panel, set the Mode (you'll usually use Normal). If you're cloning into a blank layer, set Sample to Current & Below.

4 Adjust the Hardness setting. In most cases you'll want a low value to create a feathered edge that blends better.

5 Set opacity and flow as required.

6 Use the square bracket keys ([and]) to match the size of the brush to the task.

7 Option | Alt-click on a source area to set a starting point for the Clone Stamp to sample from.

8 Use the Brush Preview to align any elements that need to match as you clone.

9 Press down the mouse button and paint to apply the cloning. A crosshair appears to show the location of the pixels that are being copied. Watch to make sure the crosshair does not move into a part of the image you don't want.

10 Optional: resize the brush and load new sources to clone and clean up other areas of the image.

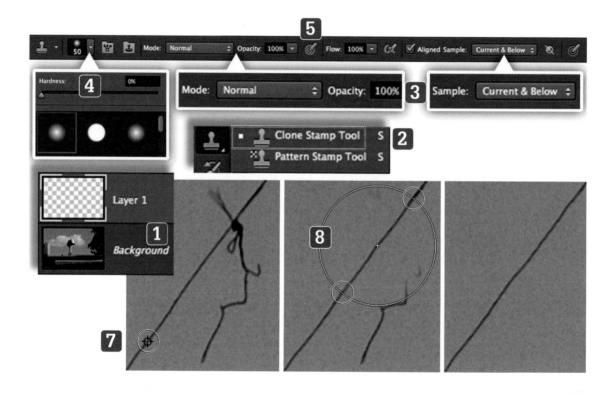

HOT TIP: You can zoom in to get a closer view of your work, but be careful: if you zoom in too much, you'll find yourself repairing things that won't show up in your print, much less on the Web. The same goes for the Healing Brush and Spot Healing Brush, which we'll cover in the next section.

Use the Healing Brush and the Spot Healing Brush

The Healing Brush tool is a mainstay of retouching. Like the Clone Stamp, it transcribes pixels from one part of an image to another, but it also lightens, darkens and adjusts the colour of the copied information to match its new surroundings. Its effect is to essentially copy the texture from one area of an image and apply it to the colour of the area you're healing. You can heal non-destructively onto a blank layer. Unlike the Cone Stamp, the tool generally works better with a high hardness setting. A soft edge makes it more difficult for the brush to calculate how to blend colours.

The Spot Healing Brush is an automatic version of the Healing Brush designed for small spots surrounded by good information, such as sensor dust or acne on someone's skin, although it can do a surprisingly good job healing away power lines from the side of a shingled building. You simply click to apply the brush instead of loading it as you do with the Healing Brush. It's best to use the tool in Content-Aware mode.

1 Create a new blank layer, re-use an existing retouching layer, or stamp a retouching layer to apply healing into. Click the retouching layer to select it.

2 To set up the Healing Brush or Spot Healing Brush:

- Select the tool from the button panel.
- Click the Brush Picker button in the Tool Options panel. Check to see that the Hardness slider is at 100%. If you're using a graphics tablet, the size will automatically be controlled by pen pressure. You can turn it off if you like. Hit the Return key to put the Brush Picker away.
- In the Options bar, check the blending Mode (default is Normal).
- Position the brush over the item that you want to heal and use the square bracket keys – [and] – to make the brush slightly larger than the area you want to cover.

3 To apply the Healing Brush:

- In the Options bar, make sure that the circle to the left of Sampled is filled in. If you're healing into a blank layer, make sure the Sample menu reads Current & Below.

- To set a starting point to sample from, Option | Alt-click on an area that has the right texture for the area you're healing. Make sure you release the Option | Alt key after you release the mouse button.

- Now paint the area that you want to heal. Sometimes you just need to click the brush in one spot, at other times you'll need to make short strokes.

4 To apply the Spot Healing Brush:

- In the Options bar, set the Type to Content-Aware. This usually yields the best results. To spot into a blank layer, tick the box marked Sample All Layers.

- Click or make short strokes over the areas that you want to heal. Do not Option | Alt-click to load the brush first. (You'll see an error message if you do.)

Use Align

The Clone Stamp and Healing Brush, discussed earlier, both have a tick box marked Aligned in the Options bar. This is a useful feature that controls where information is copied from, and can make healing or cloning lots of small areas a much easier task.

Whenever you Option | Alt-click in the image, you set a sample point that tells the tool where to start copying from as you apply the brush. After you have set the sample point, and as soon as you hold down the mouse button somewhere in the image, a little crosshair will appear at the sample point, indicating where the brush is starting to copy. As you drag the mouse across the image, that crosshair will move in a path that parallels the movement of the brush. This behaviour is the same for the first stroke you make, whether Aligned is ticked or not.

Aligned takes effect whenever you make the second and subsequent strokes. If Aligned is turned off, the brush continues to copy from the original starting point. If Aligned is turned on, the brush will move the starting point to a new location each time you start a new stroke, based on where you moved the brush.

The preview in the brush tip can help you avoid replicating areas you don't want, but you can also turn it off in the Clone Source panel, if you need to: untick the box marked Show Overlay near the bottom of the panel.

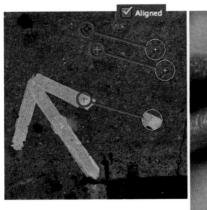 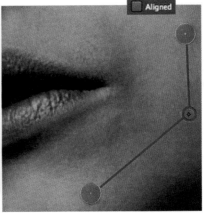

Patch and fill areas

The Patch tool is especially good for fixing moderate-size areas in a photo, and especially those that might be difficult to repair with the Healing Brush. Like the Healing Brush, it works by duplicating a part of the image and blending the duplicate into its new surroundings. You select a part of the image that you want to fix, point at an area of the image that you want to copy, and the Patch tool does the rest. The Patch tool has its own built-in Lasso tool, but you can use any method to select the problem area before you activate the Patch tool. Content-Aware Fill can sometimes do a better job of repairing your image than the Patch tool (it did for the example image). The command patches the selected area automatically. It's not consistent, but worth a try.

Unlike the Healing Brush and the Clone Stamp tools, the Patch tool and Content-Aware Fill cannot be applied to a blank layer. It's always best to duplicate the layer you want to fix or stamp a layer to work with. (See Chapter 7 for details on working with layers.) To use Content-Aware Fill, select the area you want to repair and choose Edit, Fill from the menu bar. Set the Use menu in the dialogue to Content-Aware and click OK.

To apply the Patch tool:

1 Click on the layer you wish to patch to select it.

2 Use the menu in the Tool panel button to activate the Patch tool or tap Shift + J to cycle through the tools in the button.

3 If you have not already selected the area you wish to patch, use the Patch tool Lasso to do so.

4 In the Options panel, check to see that the circle to the left of Source is filled in. If not, click on the word Source. Place the cursor over the selected area. It should have the shape shown in the illustration.

5 Press down the mouse button and drag to a different part of the image. A copy of the selected shape will follow the cursor and the original selection area will show a preview of what the patch will look like.

6 When you find an area that produces a suitable patch, release the mouse button.

7 The selection will remain active after you apply the patch. Use Command | Ctrl + H to hide the selection and evaluate your results, then use it again to restore the marching ants. You can apply the patch to a different area or use Command | Ctrl + D (menu: Select, Deselect) to release the selection.

8 The Patch tool doesn't always do a perfect job. You'll often clean up the edges with additional small patches or one of the Healing Brush tools.

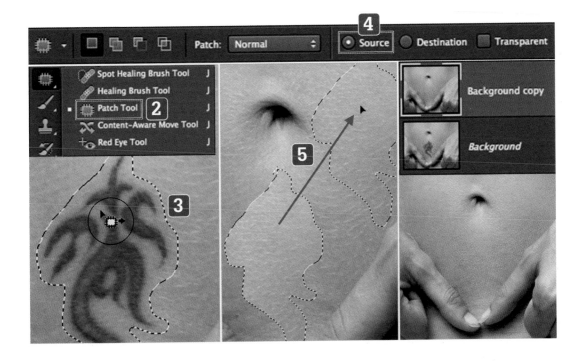

 HOT TIP: The Patch setting in CS6 now has a Content-Aware mode that can sometimes produce better results than Normal mode. The Content-Aware Move tool is new in Photoshop CS6 and works much like the Patch tool in reverse. You could use it to relocate the tattoo in the example image, instead of covering it.

Soften wrinkles

The aesthetics of retouching is a matter of personal taste and varies widely. Some people insist on having all their wrinkles removed, but that generally produces an unnatural look. An alternative is to reduce the appearance of 'character lines' without removing them completely. You can use the Clone Stamp to create a smoothed-out version of someone's skin and then fade the retouching a bit to restore some of the original texture beneath. In this example, we'll copy the area we want to repair into its own layer so that we can use the Clone Stamp with a blending mode.

1 Make a loose selection around the area that you want to soften and use Command | Ctrl + J to copy the selection to a new layer.

2 To knock down the shadows that make up the lines, use a small Clone Stamp in Lighten mode. Set Sample to Current & Below. You can build slowly by setting the Opacity to the range of 30–40%.

3 Brush over the dark lines. You can use Aligned, but make sure you Option | Alt-click from time to time to change the sampling location. Keep the source very close to the brush and copy from slightly lighter skin to lessen the wrinkle lines.

4 To burnish the area, set the Clone Stamp to Normal mode, keeping the flow and opacity low. Increase the brush size slightly. Option | Alt-click to load a source, pass over an area, then load a different source and pass back over the same area.

5 When the lines are sufficiently removed, you can reduce the opacity of the retouching layer until some of the lines return in a subdued way.

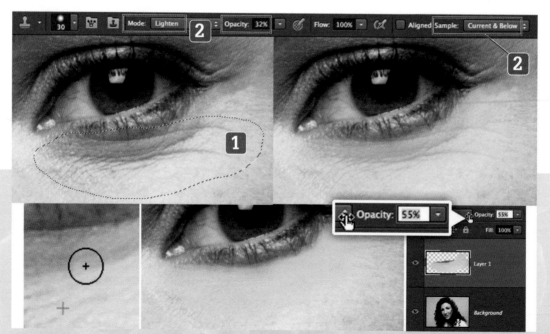

Reshape with the Liquify filter

The Liquify filter is very handy for re-sculpting things, whether it's an arm that's too thin, a bulge that's too thick, or hair that needs a little extra volume in places. With a little imagination, you'll be amazed at the applications you can find for it. As you edit your image, the tool records a mesh that is automatically saved for the next time you use the filter. So, when you edit a layer with a mask, you can reapply the filter to the mask so that they match up. You can also save the mesh to disk for reuse at any time, even on another computer. The filter performs a destructive edit, so it's best to apply it to a duplicate or stamped layer.

1 Select Filter, Liquify from the menu. The Liquify dialogue will appear.

2 Tick the Advanced Mode box to reveal the full feature set.

3 To use the Forward Warp tool: if you're trying to be subtle, the idea is to spread the distortion over a wide area.
- Select a low brush pressure (i.e. 10 or less) and a broad brush – adjust the brush size with the square bracket keys ([and]).
- Using short to medium strokes, slowly push the edges of the part of the body that you want to reshape.

4 Optional: tick the Show Backdrop box and adjust the opacity to see how your warp fits with the image.

5 Optional: use the Freeze Mask and Thaw Mask tools to protect areas from being reshaped.

6 Optional: try Pucker, Bloat and the other reshaping tools.

7 Optional: to start again, click Restore All to clear all your changes.

8 Optional: click Save Mesh and use the system dialogue to save the mesh to disk.

9 Click the OK button to commit your changes.

10 To reapply the filter, select a new item to alter (e.g. a mask thumbnail) and use one of the following methods:

- Liquify will now appear at the very top of the Filter menu. Select that item (Command | Ctrl + F) to apply the transformation without opening the dialogue.
- Select the original menu item (Shift + Command | Ctrl + X) to reopen the dialogue and use Load Last Mesh or click Load Mesh to retrieve a saved mesh. Click OK to commit the changes

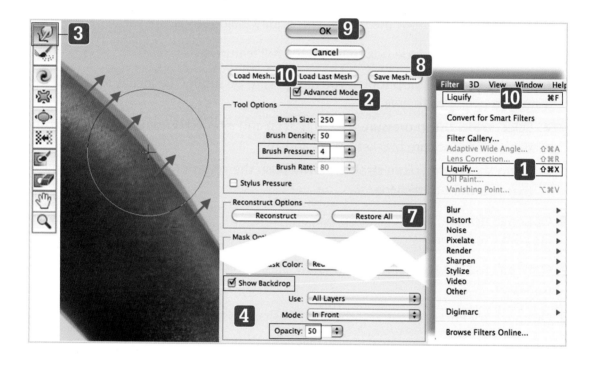

HOT TIP: The Liquify tool can warp whatever surrounds the thing you're reshaping. If you use it on a person who is standing in front of something with an obviously straight edge or a strong pattern, you might have to extract the person onto their own layer to apply Liquify and then patch or fill the underlying layer to make it believable. Content-Aware Fill can sometimes be useful for fixing patterns in such cases.

Use smart objects

An ongoing theme in this chapter has been to adopt a strategy of duplicating or stamping a layer for use with destructive editing tools such as the Patch tool: if you need to redo the patch, you can make a fresh copy of the layer and apply the tool again. A number of Photoshop features can operate on smart objects, which effectively automate that process for you and provide some additional options.

A smart object's thumbnail shows a double document icon in its lower right corner. It contains a rendered version of the layer that appears inside your main Photoshop document along with an unedited off-screen master copy (its contents). Once you convert a layer to a smart object, it no longer behaves like a pixel layer. You can think of a smart object as an embedded document that can contain layers, groups or even other smart objects. As a result, there are some considerations in editing and duplicating them, and there are a few commands (such as the Liquify filter discussed in the previous section) that cannot be applied to them.

1 To create a smart object in Photoshop, select an item in the Layers panel and then do any of the following:

- Control-click | Right-click on the label area (not the thumbnail) and choose Convert to Smart Object from the menu.
- Choose Layer, Smart Objects, Convert to Smart Object from the menu bar.

2 To open an image as a smart object from Camera Raw, hold down the Shift key to convert the Open Image button into Open Object and click. You can also open the Workflow Options dialogue and tick the box marked Open in Photoshop as Smart Objects.

3 To edit the contents (the master copy) of a smart object:

- Double-click the smart object thumbnail. You may see a warning about saving the file. Click OK. (Smart objects from Camera Raw will reopen in Camera Raw.)
- The contents will open in a new tab. Edit the file as you like and then choose File, Save (Command | Ctrl + S) from the menu bar.

- The file should simply save. If you see the Save As dialogue, click Cancel, choose Layer, Flatten Image from the menu bar, then Command | Ctrl + S.
- Close the tab and return to your main document. The rendered version of the smart object will automatically update.

4 To create a duplicate smart object, select a smart object and use Command | Ctrl + J or drag it to the New Layer icon at the bottom of the Layers panel. Duplicated smart objects share a common master copy. All duplicates will update when you edit their contents, as in Layer 2 of the example.

5 To create an independent copy of a smart object, control-click | Right-click in the label area and choose New Smart Object via Copy from the menu. Layer 3 of the example was edited after an independent copy was created.

6 To convert a smart object back into a conventional layer, control-click | Right-click on the label side of the layer and select Rasterize Layer from the menu.

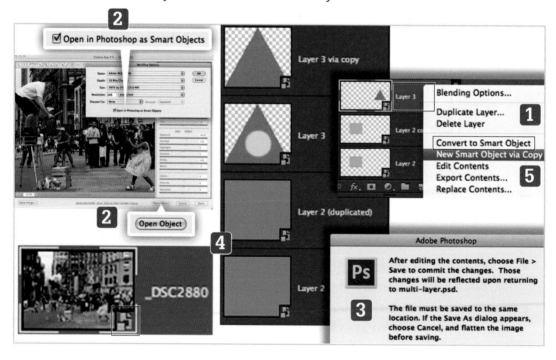

Use smart filters

Selecting Filter, Convert for Smart Filters from the menu bar is another way to create smart objects and it hints at the relationship between smart objects and smart filters: when you apply a filter to a smart object, the result is a smart filter. One great advantage of smart filters is that you can double-check or revise your settings simply by double-clicking in the Layers panel. Another advantage becomes clear when you apply more than one filter to the same object. You can't apply the Liquify filter to a smart object, but you can apply Puppet Warp, and when you do, the smart object will remember the state of your mesh and location of your pins.

To make a smart filter, use any method to create a smart object, then apply one or more filters to it. Things to bear in mind when working with filters: a few filters (Field, Iris, Tilt-Shift and Lens Blur, along with Liquify) cannot be applied to smart objects, and a number of filters work only in 8-bits-per-channel mode. For the example shown here, a photo was opened as a smart object in 16-bit mode from Camera Raw. The Adaptive Wide Angle filter was applied, followed by Smart Sharpen. The filters stack beneath the smart object, with the first filter applied at the bottom. Smart filters include a filter mask, which works just like a layer mask but controls where the filters are applied within the image. You can also add a layer mask, if necessary.

1. Click the eyeball icon next to an individual smart filter (e.g. Smart Sharpen) to toggle its effect.

2. Click the eyeball to the left of the filter mask to toggle all filters.

3. Double-click the name of an individual smart filter to open its settings.

4. Double-click the slider icon on the right edge of a smart filter to open its Blending Options dialogue. The dialogue allows you to reduce the strength of the effect with opacity and change its blending mode.

5. Drag filter names up and down the list to change the order of application (e.g. blur before noise vs noise before blur).

6 Optional: paint in the filter mask to constrain the application of the filters. All filters share the mask.

7 If you don't need the filter mask, you can remove it to free up space. Control-click | Right-click on the mask and select Delete Filter Mask from the menu.

8 Click the disclosure triangle on the right edge of the smart object to hide or reveal your smart filters.

9 To delete a smart filter, Control-click | Right-click on the name of the Smart Filter and select Delete Smart Filter from the menu.

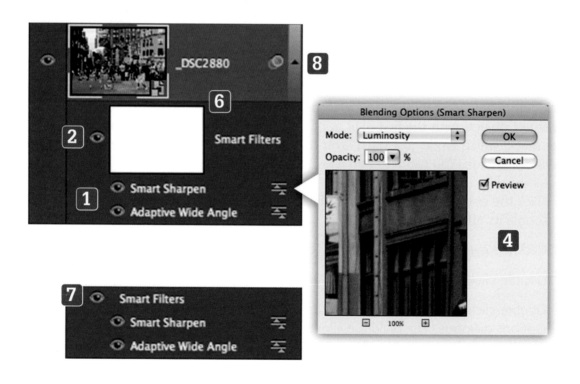

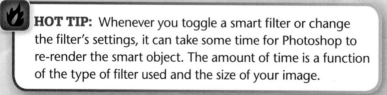

HOT TIP: Whenever you toggle a smart filter or change the filter's settings, it can take some time for Photoshop to re-render the smart object. The amount of time is a function of the type of filter used and the size of your image.

Use Free Transform

Select Edit, Free Transform (Command | Ctrl + T) from the menu bar to activate the feature. You can think of it as an umbrella command for a suite of transformation modes. Use control handles in the image or the Options bar: type in a field or scrub (drag the cursor across) field labels to enter values.

1 Shift-drag corners of the transform frame to scale proportionately; drag corners to stretch and reshape.

2 Option | Alt-drag the handles to expand or contract around the centre. Use Shift + Option | Alt to centre circles and squares.

3 Control-click | Right-click inside the handles and use the menu to select a transformation mode.

4 Drag outside the transform handles to rotate; reposition the reference point to rotate around a specific axis.

5 In Perspective mode, drag the corner handles to shift perspective and drag the centre handles to skew.

6 Click the icon in the Options bar to switch to or from Warp mode. Use pre-sets or drag handles and mesh lines to warp.

7 To reposition via the Options bar:
- Click the points in the reference point locator (default is the centre of the object) and enter values into the X and Y (horizontal and vertical) fields to position elements precisely.
- Click the delta (triangle) icon to reposition relative to the current position (instead of the upper left corner of the document), e.g. + 10 pixels on the X-axis.

 HOT TIP: If you think you might transform a pixel layer more than once, you can protect it from cumulative degradation by converting it to a smart object before you apply Free Transform. For example, if you're not sure what size an item needs to be, you might shrink the layer and decide to enlarge it later.

 DID YOU KNOW?
The menu command Select, Transform Selection affords the same set of features for modifying selections without affecting the pixels.

8 To scale via the Options bar, enter W(idth) and H(eight) into the Options bar to scale numerically. Activate the chain icon to link W and H for proportional scaling. Enter abbreviations for scale: px, in, cm and % for pixels, inches, centimetres and per cent.

- Interpolation controls how the scaling is done. Bicubic is generally the best all-round method. The new Bicubic Automatic will select a method depending on whether you're scaling up or down.

9 You can enter an angle into the Rotation, H(orizontal skew) or V(ertical skew) fields.

10 Hit Return | Enter to commit the transformation, or Esc to cancel.

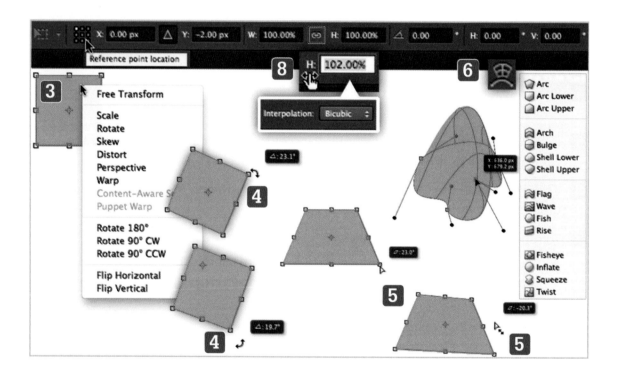

 HOT TIP: If you make a selection in a pixel layer before activating Free Transform, the command will transform the selected pixels. The same modes are available as when you transform an entire layer. When you commit the transformation, your changes are merged into the layer. It can be a good alternative to cloning.

14 Add text

Introduction

Photoshop offers a rich set of tools for working with text. Even if your prime interest in Photoshop is working with images, there are a number of situations where you may want to combine images and text – adding a copyright notice to the bottom of your images or creating a promotional piece, for example. In such cases, you will find Photoshop's Type tools to be very useful. If your interest in graphic design is stronger, you're likely to appreciate Photoshop's typographic capabilities even more.

Pixel editing is one of the things that Photoshop does best, but it handles text as vector outlines that remain editable unless you rasterise the text (convert it to pixels). Because of this, you can cleanly scale and transform your text to any size. Photoshop CS6 Extended will even let you easily render your text in 3D with qualities such as translucence and reflectivity.

Use Type tools

You'll generally use the Horizontal Type tool to place text into your document. Its button in the Tools panel also houses the Vertical Type tool and two Type Mask tools, but you probably won't use any of them. Even if you ultimately need vertical text, you can click the orientation button on the left side of the Options bar at any time, and we'll look at a better alternative to the Type Mask tools later in this chapter.

Beyond the controls in the Options bar, you can further refine text with the Character and Paragraph panels. Photoshop CS6 introduces new Paragraph and Character Styles panels, which can be useful if you expect to do a lot of typography in Photoshop.

Here's a simple overview of working with text. Tap T to activate the Type tool or select it from the menu in the Tools panel. Configure the tool as outlined below. Place the cursor and type your text. Hit Enter (not Return) to commit the text. Photoshop will place your text in a new type layer. Once the layer is created, you can add layer styles, clip images to it, apply the Free Transform commands, even convert it to 3D.

1 Configure the Type tool in the Options bar:
- Set the font, style and size.
- Optional: select an anti-aliasing method.
- Set the alignment.
- To change the colour, click the swatch to open the Color Picker.

2 Click the icon in the Options bar to open the Character Panel:
- Set leading (line spacing).
- Use tracking to stretch or shorten individual lines – this is good for making ragged text look less ragged.
- Use kerning to manage overlap between character pairs such as V and A.
- One use for shifting the baseline is to adjust text that has been applied to a path.

3 Optional: click the Paragraph tab to control justification, margins, indenting, and space before and after paragraphs.

4 Optional: click the Warp button to transform the text. After warping, the text will remain editable.

5 Optional: define Paragraph and Character styles.

 HOT TIP: Perspective is one transformation mode that cannot be applied to live text. If you convert the text to a smart object, though, you can apply the perspective transformation and still open the smart object to edit the text if you need to.

Make straight-line text

Use this method to add short bits of text to your image. There is a critical bit about editing text on a Mac: this is the one place where Return and Enter do not do the same thing. When you hit Return, it tells Photoshop that you want to add a new line. When you hit Enter, it tells Photoshop that you have finished editing the text.

1 Activate the Type tool. The cursor will change to an I-beam.

2 In the Options panel, check the font, point size and text alignment.

3 Click (do not drag) on the canvas to place an insertion point.

4 Type some text. Notice the blinking cursor.

5 Hit the Enter key, click the tick in the Options bar, or click on a thumbnail in the Layers panel (you can click on the layer's own thumbnail) to commit the text. Hit Esc to cancel.

6 Notice that the new text layer takes its name from its content.

7 You can click the Type tool in another part of the image to start another straight-line type layer.

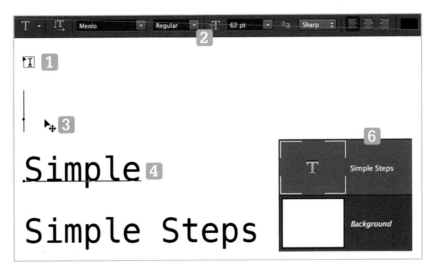

HOT TIP: While the Type tool is active, you cannot use the letter keys to access other tools in the Tools panel because the tool sees it all as normal typing. Don't forget to commit the text.

ALERT: A pitfall of working with the Type tool is that you can click to start some text and then click elsewhere and end up with blank type layers. Just click to select the unwanted layers in the Layers panel and hit the Delete | Backspace key to get rid of them.

Make wrapping text

When you drag the Type tool, you define a box to hold wrapping text. The initial size and shape of the box are not critical since the box can be reshaped later.

1. Activate the Type tool, drag a rectangular shape with the mouse pointer, then release the mouse button.

2. Type text into the box. When it hits the edge, you will see it wrap.

3. Use the handles on the text box to reshape it. Notice that the text re-flows to fit the box and that it is clipped when the box is too small.

HOT TIP: Hold down the Option | Alt key as you drag the handles to shrink or expand the text box from the centre.

4. Optional: click inside the text to place the cursor and hit Return to add paragraph breaks.

5. Hit the Enter key, click the tick in the Options bar, or click any thumbnail in the Layers panel to commit your edits.

6. You can drag the Type tool in another part of the image to start a new wrapping text layer or click to create a new straight-line type layer.

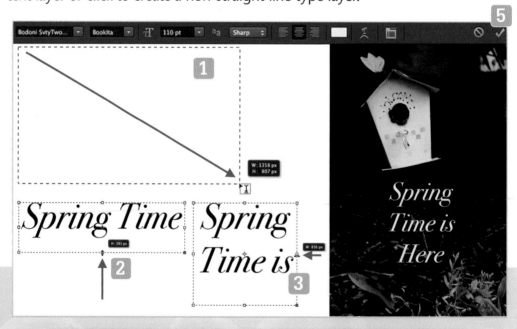

ALERT: Commit your text before trying to activate other Photoshop features. As long as you see the control handles for the text box, keyboard shortcuts and other Photoshop commands (including opening files) will not be available. Photoshop may not respond at all, or it may beep.

Re-edit committed text

Once you have committed a Type layer, you can edit it at any time. If the text is wrapping text, you can also reshape the box when you reopen the text for editing.

1 To begin re-editing:

- Activate the Type tool and position it over the text you want to edit. The cursor will change shape. Click or drag inside the text. The Type tool will automatically select the layer and open the text box.

2 For wrapping text, drag any of the handles around the edge to reshape the text box. Drag outside the corners of the box to rotate the text.

3 Edit either type of text as in any standard text editor:

- Double-click to select a word.
- Triple-click to select a line.
- Click to place the cursor and then Shift-click to select all text between the two clicks.
- Once the blinking cursor is inside the text or any part of the text is selected, you can also use Command | Ctrl+A to select all text.
- Control-click | Right-click on the selected text to show a contextual menu that includes spell checking, search and replace, and anti-aliasing options.

4 Hit Enter to commit the text when you are satisfied.

Make typographic adjustments

The Options bar provides easy access to the most frequently used typographic tools, and the Character panel extends them. The Paragraphs panel is most useful for laying out wrapping text with multiple paragraphs. Some editing options are listed below.

1 To show the Character panel, either click on the Character panel button in the Options bar or select Window, Character from the menu bar.

2 To change point size, use the size control in either the Options bar or the Character panel. Type into the field or scrub (drag the mouse pointer) across the label.

3 To change text colour, click on the colour swatch in the Options bar or the Character panel to open the Color Picker.

4 Use the buttons to the left of the colour swatch to change text alignment.

5 Select all or part of a single line of text and adjust the Tracking in the Character panel to shorten or lengthen the line by changing the spacing between letters.

6 Click the Paragraph tab to activate the panel. Use it to adjust alignment, justification, margins, first-line indent and padding for each paragraph.

7 To warp text, click the Warp button in the Options bar, choose a warp style from the menu and adjust the settings in the dialogue. To remove the warp, reopen the dialogue and choose None from the style menu.

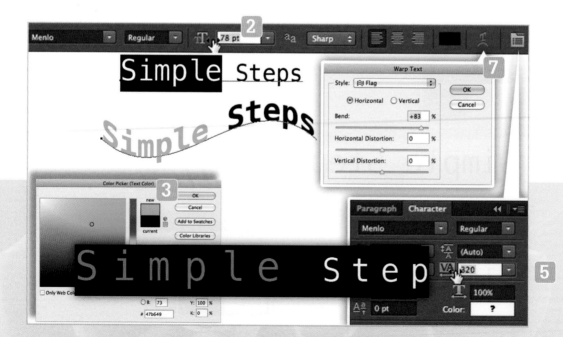

Create a watermark

A frequent application of text in photography is adding a watermark or logo, and a frequent problem is that the type blends with parts of the image and becomes unreadable. Dark text will get lost against dark parts of the image, while light text will disappear in the highlights. A good strategy is to combine the two, surrounding dark text with a light halo. One way to address that is to apply a layer style such as Outer Glow to the text. It's often even more effective when you use it with a blending mode, and less obtrusive with reduced opacity. For the example, the final watermark was integrated by setting the blending mode to Overlay and reducing the opacity to 25%. The Screen and Soft Light blending modes often work well for creating watermarks.

1 Add your text with the Type tool.

2 Select the layer and choose Outer Glow from the Layer Style (*f*x) menu at the bottom of the Layers panel.

3 Adjust the settings for the glow as you like:

- In the Structure section, click the swatch to use the Color Picker. A white or near-white glow is generally best for this application. Setting the Blend Mode to Screen sometimes helps to create separation.

- In the Elements section, varying the size with the Softer Technique setting works well.

- In the Quality section, click the blue button with the triangle (not the contour thumbnail) to open the contour picker. The Gaussian (upper right) and Half Round (lower left) contours work well for this application. Adjust the Range to create a diffuse surround.

4 Click OK to save the settings and close the dialogue.

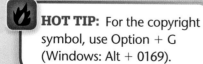

HOT TIP: For the copyright symbol, use Option + G (Windows: Alt + 0169).

DID YOU KNOW?

It sometimes helps to reduce the opacity of the glow or set the glow to a different blending mode. You can double-click the Outer Glow label, reopen the dialogue and edit the style.

Clip an image to text

In Chapter 10, a clipping mask was used to attach an adjustment to a single layer. In this example, we'll look at a different application of the same principle: stylised text will serve as the base layer to mask an image.

1 Edit your text. For this feature to work well, you want your text to provide a good amount of surface for the image to show through: try thick, bold, slab or sans serif fonts such as Rockwell, Egyptian and Soho Gothic.

- The font in the example is Adabi MT Condensed Extra Bold.
- The text was entered over the background layer as a wrapping, centre-aligned block. Free Transform was then used to scale it. The line spacing was then reduced and Free Transform was used again to stretch it vertically.

2 To use the type layer as a base for the clipping mask, drag it directly beneath the image layer. If the image is in the background layer, you'll need to convert it to a normal layer first. Hold down the Option | Alt key and double-click on the thumbnail to convert it to Layer 0.

3 To clip the image to the text, hover the mouse pointer over the dividing line between the two layers and hold down the Option | Alt button. The icon will change to indicate that the layers are about to be clipped together. Click to clip the layers. A bent arrow icon will appear to show that the layer is clipped to the one beneath it, and its thumbnail will indent.

4 After clipping, the text will be surrounded by transparent pixels (you'll see a grey checkerboard pattern). A white background was added to the example:

- Click the top layer and then click the New Layer icon at the bottom of the Layers panel.
- Select Edit, Fill from the menu bar. Choose a colour and click OK to apply.
- Drag the white layer (Layer 1 in the illustration) beneath the type layer.

5 Optional: click the image layer to select it, activate the Move tool and drag the image layer so that interesting or salient bits show through the text.

6 Optional: add final adjustments:

- In the example, some of the letters did not separate well from the white background. A 50% grey stroke was added to the type layer. Click the type layer and select Stroke from the *f*x menu at the bottom of the Layers panel.

- A Curves adjustment layer was also added to create a bit more contrast.

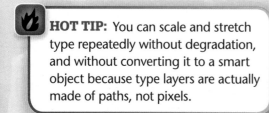

HOT TIP: You can scale and stretch type repeatedly without degradation, and without converting it to a smart object because type layers are actually made of paths, not pixels.

15 Resize, resample and sharpen

Introduction

This brief chapter is about image size and quality. Whenever you deal with making your image appear larger or smaller in print or on the Web, you'll visit the question of resampling. The second question you'll concern yourself with is whether or not to sharpen.

If you're making an image for the Web or an email attachment you're likely to resample. If you're printing, the megapixel size of your camera will determine the largest print you can make without resampling. As you decrease the resolution of the print, its size increases, but when the resolution gets too low, the quality will suffer. You can resample to increase the resolution, but it can also make the image look softer, so there are practical limits to how big you can make prints.

When you resample, Photoshop performs a set of calculations to synthesise new pixels in your image, changing the number of pixels and the amount of space the file takes on your hard drive. That's a fundamental change, so you'll always want to save the resulting file with a new name or as a copy after resampling.

Sharpening is really a misnomer. It doesn't bring out-of-focus elements into focus; rather, it increases the contrast around edges, making some things seem sharper. We'll look at one form of sharpening that's useful for bringing out detail and shine, and a second that's particularly good for sharpening for output.

Use the resize option

The size of your prints is only partially determined by your camera's megapixels. The other factor is the size of the pixels you print – the resolution, measured in dpi or dots/cm – which also affects image quality. You can use the Image Size dialogue to see the relationship between print size and resolution.

There are a few resolution values to be aware of: 240 dpi (95 dots/cm) produces high-quality prints with inkjet printers, while 300 dpi (118 dots/cm) is industry standard for laser printing. Print quality is compromised below a resolution of 150 dpi (60 dots/cm). You'll often see resolution cited in ppi or pixels/cm as well. The two are interchangeable; ppi generally refers to images onscreen, while dpi refers to printed images. With a 10-megapixel camera, you can print up to about 27 cm by 41 cm (11" × 16") without having to resample.

The example on the left shows how reducing the resolution from 300 to 240 ppi increased the width of the print by more than 6 cm. Chances are you'd need at least a magnifying glass to find any difference in quality. The example on the right shows how the new Nikon D800's 4912 × 7360 (36-megapixel) images will make 52 × 78 cm (20" × 30") prints at 240 dpi (95 dots/cm), while a typical size 871 × 1280-pixel image downloaded from the Web can produce only a 15 × 22 cm (6" × 9") print at 150 dpi (60 dots/cm).

1 To open the dialogue, choose Image, Image Size from the menu bar. The Image Size dialogue will appear.

2 Make sure the box marked Resample Image near the bottom of the dialogue is not ticked.

3 Enter a width or a height that best fits the paper you will be printing on. It's best to leave somewhere between 1 cm and ½ inch margin on the longest dimension.

4 Note the resolution. If the number falls well below 240 pixels/inch (600 pixels/cm), you should consider resampling.

5 Click OK.

6 If you plan to regularly print at this size, save your file and these dimensions will be stored in the file.

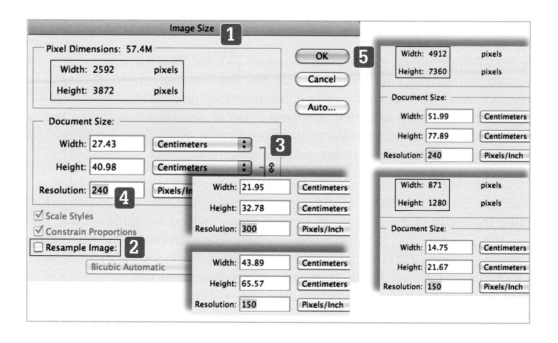

Resample images

When you resample an image, Photoshop literally takes your image apart and rebuilds it. Increasing the file dimensions is called up sampling, and it works by spreading the pixels apart to span the new size and synthesising new pixels to fill in the gaps. When you make the image smaller by down sampling, Photoshop overlaps the pixels and calculates new pixels based on the overlapping colours.

Photoshop actually has three methods for resampling images. The Image Size dialogue is the main tool for changing the size of files, but Fit Image is a simpler tool that is particularly useful for down sampling images. You can also resample images as you export them with the File, Save for Web command.

As discussed in the previous section, you'll probably want to resample to 240 or 300 dpi, though you can also probably get away with 150 dpi (95, 118 or 60 dots/cm, respectively) for a large print. When you resample an image for the Web, only the pixel dimensions are relevant because (unlike a printer) the content cannot change the resolution of the user's screen.

1 When resampling for the Web, you can select File, Automate, Fit Image from the menu bar. Enter size constraints to define the maximum dimensions for the image. Click OK. Photoshop will scale the image to fit inside the constraints.

2 To use the Image Size dialogue: select Image, Image Size from the menu bar to open the dialogue.

3 For the Web, enter a width or height in pixels. The other dimension will be calculated for you.

4 For printing, you may not need to resample. Check the resolution first. Untick the Resample Image box and enter the dimensions you want to print.

- If the resolution drops below 150 dpi, tick the Resample Image box and enter the resolution you wish to use.

5 If you do want to resample, make sure that the boxes labelled Resample Image and Constrain Proportions are ticked. If you enter percentage values in the Pixel Dimensions, the results will appear in the Document Size section.

6 Optional: adjust the interpolation menu at the bottom of the dialogue. Photoshop will select a method for you when it is set to Bicubic Automatic. Otherwise, use Bicubic.

7 Click OK to resample.

8 Once the image is resampled by either method, you can print it or save the file as a JPEG for email or the Web.

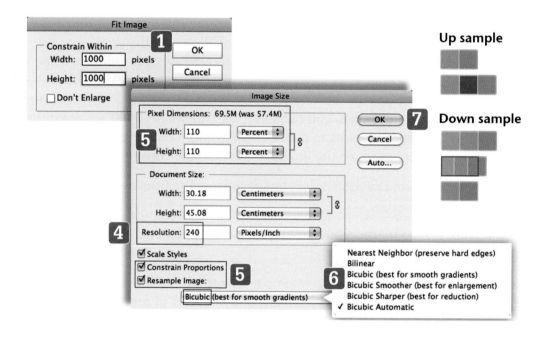

ALERT: Up sampling injects filler into your image, and down sampling remixes and throws pixels away. You never want to replace your original with a resampled version, because even the slightest resampling degrades your image somewhat. You should use Save As when you save a resampled file. When you need to increase the file size substantially, it's often helpful to up sample in several steps of 110%, instead of all at once.

Sharpen with the High Pass filter

High Pass sharpening could be called creative sharpening. While it's useful as a tool for any kind of edge enhancement, it is best used for emphasising the edges and the shine of things such as jewellery, hair or to catch lights in someone's hair. Sharpening for output is best left to Smart Sharpen. Since this type of enhancement is typically added after you've done some retouching and tonal work, the example uses it with a stamped layer.

1 Begin by stamping a layer at the top of your layer stack to which to apply sharpening (see Chapter 7).

2 Be sure the stamped layer is active and select Filter, Other, High Pass from the menu bar. The High Pass dialogue box will appear.

3 Move the Radius slider in small increments and notice when the features you want to enhance appear as faint lines in the main image window (don't worry about what you can or can't see in the dialogue window). You can increase the radius slightly from that point, but eventually you will get unsightly haloes. In most cases, you will find that a radius between 5 and 15 works best.

4 Click the OK button. You'll see an odd, grey image.

5 Choose Image, Adjustments, Desaturate from the menu bar. This eliminates any potential colour fringes that can come from the High Pass effect.

6 Change the blending mode of the layer to Overlay. The sharpening effect should be apparent.

7 For a before and after view, toggle the visibility of the layer by clicking its eyeball a few times.

8 Possible ways to further refine the effect:

- Reduce the opacity of the layer.
- Use Soft Light blending mode for a reduced effect, or try Hard Light or Vivid Light for a stronger effect.
- Increase the effect by duplicating the layer.
- Select the sharpening layer and Option | Alt-click on the Add layer mask icon to add a black mask. The sharpening will disappear from the entire image. Paint with white to restore the effect to specific areas. Use a soft brush at reduced Opacity/Flow for a controlled, gradual build-up.

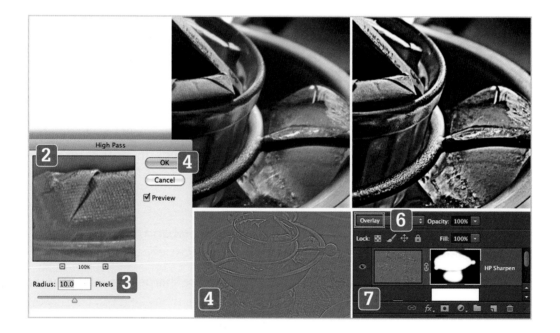

Use Smart Sharpen

The biggest problem with sharpening is that many people overdo it, producing images that have harsh highlights, unsightly haloes or brittle-looking details. The trick is to find the appropriate radius and then dial in the amount. That starts with viewing your image at the proper resolution as you sharpen. Sharpening for print often looks like it's too much on screen because it is, but it needs to be that aggressive to hold up in your print. The technique outlined below makes it easy to apply sharpening effectively.

1 If you're sharpening for the Web, resample the image to the size you plan to save and then view it at 100%.

2 If you're sharpening for print:

- Make sure that you have calculated and set your screen resolution as described in Chapter 8 or set the preference to a more accurate 100 dpi (menu: Photoshop, Preferences, Units & Rulers).
- Select View, Print size from the menu bar.

3 If your entire image does not fit on screen, you can hit the tab key to temporarily hide the panels and free up space. Position the image so that you can see the effect of sharpening on a salient part. Hold down the H key and press the mouse button to engage Bird's Eye View. Drag the box to the part of the image you want to use, release the mouse button and then release the H key.

4 Stamp a layer at the top of your layer stack to contain your sharpening (see Chapter 7). Make sure the sharpening layer is selected.

5 To open the dialogue, select Filter, Sharpen, Smart Sharpen. Position the dialogue so that you can see your image and the dialogue controls. You can push the dialogue's preview off-screen. You'll be evaluating the image directly.

6 Make sure the Remove option is set to Lens Blur and leave More Accurate unticked.

7 To determine the radius:

- Move the Radius slider all the way to the left — 0.1 pixels.

! ALERT: Be careful about sharpening skin – it brings out pores and texture. The 'More Accurate' option sharpens textures even more aggressively. You can use a layer mask to hide the sharpening on skin – use the Color Range command to assist in selecting the skin and then invert the mask. See Chapters 11 and 12 for details.

- Move the Amount slider all the way to the right, so that the amount reads 500%.
- Now, slowly increase radius. You can click in the Radius box and adjust in 0.1-pixel increments with the up or down arrow keys. Hold the Shift key and tap the keys for 1-pixel increments. Tap the P key to toggle the preview as you adjust the radius.
- At some point, the sharpening will begin to make the image look somewhat brittle. In the example photo, that was around 7 pixels. Back off that setting by approximately ½ pixel. This is your sharpening radius.

8 Set the amount for screen sharpening. Move the Amount slider to 100% and then increase to an acceptable level. Click in the Amount field and use the arrow keys for 1% increments and Shift + the arrow keys for 10% increments. Tap P to toggle the preview and evaluate. Once you determine the amount, sharpening for screen is nearly complete.

9 If you're sharpening for print, triple the radius setting (e.g. 6.5 for screen = 19.5 for print). The actual radius to use for print will vary depending upon the paper that you use, but this is a good rule-of-thumb setting. If you're making critical prints, you'll want to make test prints with different sharpening settings.

10 To finalise the sharpening:

- Click the OK button to apply the effect and immediately select Edit, Fade Smart Sharpen from the menu bar.
- In the Fade dialogue, set the mode to Luminosity and click OK. This will remove colour artefacts that the sharpening process produces.
- If you've hidden your panels, hit the tab key to restore them.
- Toggle the visibility of your sharpen layer to compare before and after.

16 Make prints

Introduction

When Photoshop manages colours, it translates the colour numbers in your image into the corresponding numbers for the printer profile. For the most accurate colour matching between your screen and printer, it's best to work with a display that has been calibrated and profiled. If the brightness of your screen is set very high, you will consistently find that your prints come out dark. Turning down the brightness may make your work look less dazzling on screen, but you'll get better print matching. See Chapter 4 for more info on colour management.

The examples in this chapter feature the drivers from the Epson 2880 printer. Because printer drivers can look very different by make, model and operating system, your printer driver's screens may look different, but the principles and often the language used will be exactly the same. Manufacturers often update their printer drivers, especially after Microsoft and Apple release new system software. Check the manufacturer's website periodically for updates.

When you are ready to print, your first concern is setting the proper print size and resolution. Depending upon your needs, you may resample the image to make a larger print (see Chapter 15). After that, the question of sharpening arises. Whether or not to sharpen is a matter of personal preference, and the best time to apply sharpening, if at all, is after the print resolution is set. The next consideration is the colour spaces and bit depth you wish to work with. When you have an accurate printer profile, having Photoshop manage the colours will produce the best results, and you can print from wide-gamut colour spaces like Adobe RGB and ProPhoto RGB (which absolutely requires 16-bit printing).

As of the Snow Leopard release on Mac OS, your printer driver will automatically turn off its colour management when it sees that Photoshop is managing colours. A poor printer profile will produce substandard results. In that case, you can let the printer manage the colours. Most will give good results with a file that has been converted to sRGB, and Epson's printers also support Adobe RGB. In some cases, you'll need to switch on Epson's colour management when you select the Printer Manages Colors option in Photoshop – switch to the Color Matching section of the printer driver and make sure that EPSON Color Controls is selected.

Finally, Printing often goes faster when you print from a flattened file. You can flatten the file before printing (menu: Layer, Flatten Image), then undo the flattening or close the flattened file without saving it when you've finished.

Print with Photoshop colour management

When Photoshop manages colours, it translates the colour numbers between your image and the colour space of the printer profile. With an accurate printer profile, Photoshop can outperform the printer's generic colour management and produce highly accurate colour prints. This page presents a summary of the entire process. The rest of this chapter will discuss these topics in greater detail.

1. Select File, Print from the menu bar. The Print dialogue will appear.

2. Select the printer and set the layout orientation.

3. Edit print settings (printer driver):
   - Turn off colour management.
   - Select page size and paper feed.
   - Select media type and print quality.

4. Set up Color Management (Photoshop):
   - Select Photoshop Color Management.
   - Select the printer profile and rendering intent for Photoshop Color Management.
   - Send 16-bit data when available.

5. Set page layout (position and size) parameters.

6. Check to see that your paper is properly loaded.

7. Click Print.

8. Save your file to retain the print configuration.

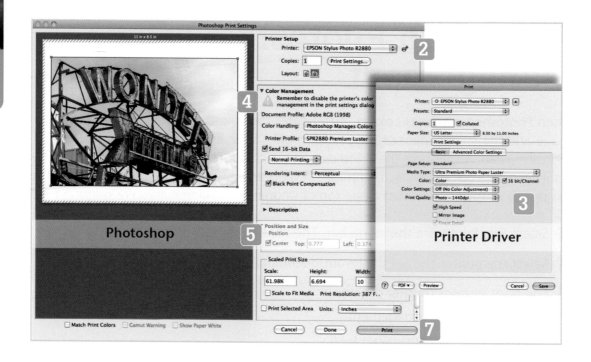

SEE ALSO: For more on using printer profiles, see Install colour profiles in Chapter 4.

Edit and save print settings

When you click the Print Settings button, you open the printer driver dialogue. Your printer driver may have a different interface than the one shown here. Check with your printer manufacturer for additional information on using its driver. Assuming that you're using one of the more recent versions of Windows or Mac OS (Snow Leopard or newer), the operating system now takes a more active role in colour management, and you probably won't have to turn off colour management in the printer driver (step 9 below) when you select Photoshop Manages Colours. However, if you're printing from a 16-bit file, you'll still have to send 16-bit data from Photoshop and turn on 16-bit printing in the driver.

When you click Save, Photoshop stores the specified printer in the document along with its driver settings. Once you save the file, Photoshop will reuse the settings without showing the printer dialogue when you choose File, Print One Copy from the menu bar.

1. Choose your printer from the menu and enter the number of copies.

2. Use the Layout (horizontal or vertical format) buttons to orient the image. Some of the image may appear clipped – that's OK for now.

3. Click Print Settings to open the print driver dialogue.

4. Select your printer and paper size from the menus. The paper size selection also determines which path to load the paper through. Use the Manual – Roll size options to feed stiffer paper and rolls through the alternative slot.

5. Select Print Settings from the menu in the middle of the dialogue. (If you don't see the menu, click the button with the triangle to expand the dialogue.)

6. Set the Media Type to match the kind of paper you are using. (If you are not sure which media type is best to use, check with your paper's manufacturer.)

7. Optional: click Advanced Color Settings for advice on which profile to use for colour management, then click Basic to return to the main screen.

8 Select Color. If you are printing from a 16-bit file, tick 16 bit/Channel (the bit-depth appears in the document title).

9 Check to see that your printer's colour controls are switched to Off (No Color Adjustment) because Photoshop is managing the colour. If your print comes out with a strong magenta cast, it's probably because you didn't turn off this setting.

10 Choose a Print Quality setting. Photo – 1440dpi works best for most situations. (You will be hard-pressed to see a difference with SuperPhoto – 2880, though it uses more ink.)

11 Optional: tick High Speed for faster bi-directional printing.

12 Click Save to store your settings in the document.

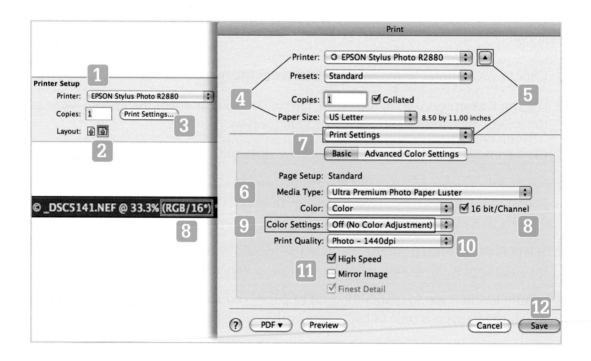

ALERT: If you see fine horizontal lines in your prints, try turning off the High Speed setting and reprinting. Some papers may require using a special paper path and some may require adjusting the platen gap. See your printer documentation for more details.

Set colour management parameters

The colour management parameters are essential for getting quality colour out of your printer. Use the disclosure triangle in the upper left corner to expand or collapse the section as required.

1 Select Photoshop Manages Colors from the Color Handling menu. The alert reminding you to disable the printer's colour management refers to step 9 in the previous section. (This feature will be automatic with recent versions of Mac OS X and Windows with many printer drivers.)

2 In the Printer Profile menu, select a profile that matches your printer and paper combination:

- The first group of profiles that appears in the menu is for the currently selected printer, but all installed colour profiles will appear in the list.
- If you're printing to an Epson printer, you can use the recommended profile (see step 7 of the previous section).

3 Select a Rendering Intent: choose either Relative Colorimetric or Perceptual.

- Even though Perceptual can shift colours in your image more, colour gradients are less likely to break down.
- Relative Colorimetric is not recommended if you are printing a ProPhoto RGB document – it will probably cause gradients to posterise into bands of flat colour.
- When in doubt, make test prints with both intents and compare the results.
- Saturation and Absolute Colorimetric are not for photography.

4 If you're printing from a 16-bit image, tick Send 16-bit Data (the bit-depth appears in the title tab).

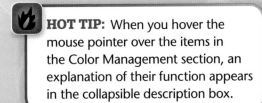

HOT TIP: When you hover the mouse pointer over the items in the Color Management section, an explanation of their function appears in the collapsible description box.

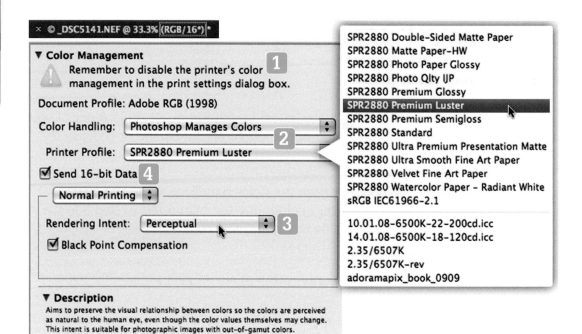

× © _DSC5141.NEF @ 33.3% (RGB/16*) *

▼ **Color Management**

⚠ Remember to disable the printer's color management in the print settings dialog box. **1**

Document Profile: Adobe RGB (1998)

Color Handling: [Photoshop Manages Colors ▼] **2**

Printer Profile: [SPR2880 Premium Luster ▼]

☑ Send 16-bit Data **4**

[Normal Printing ▼]

Rendering Intent: [Perceptual ▼] **3**

☑ Black Point Compensation

SPR2880 Double-Sided Matte Paper
SPR2880 Matte Paper-HW
SPR2880 Photo Paper Glossy
SPR2880 Photo Qlty IJP
SPR2880 Premium Glossy
SPR2880 Premium Luster
SPR2880 Premium Semigloss
SPR2880 Standard
SPR2880 Ultra Premium Presentation Matte
SPR2880 Ultra Smooth Fine Art Paper
SPR2880 Velvet Fine Art Paper
SPR2880 Watercolor Paper – Radiant White
sRGB IEC61966-2.1

10.01.08-6500K-22-200cd.icc
14.01.08-6500K-18-120cd.icc
2.35/6507K
2.35/6507K-rev
adoramapix_book_0909

▼ **Description**

Aims to preserve the visual relationship between colors so the colors are perceived as natural to the human eye, even though the color values themselves may change. This intent is suitable for photographic images with out-of-gamut colors.

WHAT DOES THIS MEAN?

Profile names: these are usually abbreviated and structured in the format [printer] [paper] [extras], e.g. SPR2880 stands for Stylus Photo R2880. Extras might include PK for photo black and MK for matte black ink.

Position, size and start the print job

Use the page layout parameters to precisely position the image on the page. You can even print a section of the image.

1 Photoshop will centre your image by default. To move your image off-centre, untick the box marked Center. Once you click in one of the position fields, you can type a value or use the up or down arrow keys or Shift plus the arrow keys to position the image on the page.

2 To set the size of your print, use either of these methods:
- Use the Units menu to set a measurement scale and type in a height, width or scale value that leaves a margin of 1 cm to ½ inch on the long dimension.
- Tick Scale to Fit Media to automatically size the image using the maximum print area.

3 To scale or position your image visually:
- Drag the edges or the corners of the box to scale the image.
- Drag inside the box to reposition on the page.

4 After you have sized your image, notice the print resolution at the bottom of the box. Resolutions of 150 ppi (60 pixels/cm) or less will produce low-quality prints. You can try resampling to increase resolution (see the previous chapter).

5 Optional: tick Print Selected Area to print part of the image.
- If you made a selection before starting to print, Photoshop will create a shield for you, otherwise drag the handles in the left and top margin to frame the area you wish to print.
- Drag inside the image to position detail inside the print selection.

 HOT TIP: In most cases, your margins will not be equal because the proportions of the sides in the image do not match the proportions of most standard paper sizes.

 HOT TIP: Edge-to-edge printing sprays ink all over the inside of your printer and causes problems. If you want clean edges, it's better to trim away the borders after your print dries.

6 Once you have positioned and sized the image, you can press Print to send the job to the printer. All your print dialogue information will be stored in your Photoshop document. Save the file to retain the settings for future use.

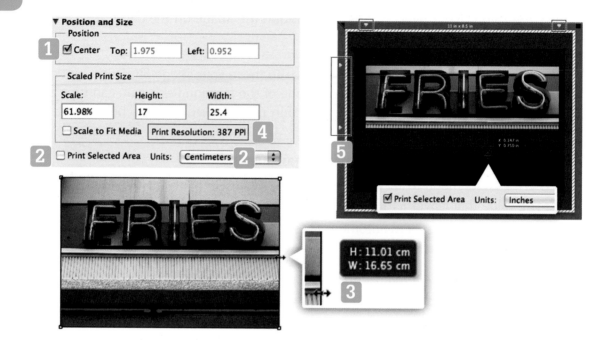

Print in black and white

As we saw in Chapter 10, a lot of 'black and white' imagery is actually colourised; such images will print best with Photoshop colour management. However, when you print from a Grayscale-mode image or use a Black & White adjustment layer to create a neutral black and white image, the printing situation changes. Depending on your printer's ability to print neutral greyscale images, you may get better results letting the printer manage the colours.

Photoshop's colour management prints all images as RGB, which will cause the printer to use any of its inks in producing the print and can potentially introduce unwanted colours into your black and white prints. Printers such as Epson's Stylus Photo R2880 and Canon's PIXMA Pro 9500 Mk II have multiple grey and black inks designed to produce exceptional black and white images with no colour cast. It's a simple matter to tell Photoshop to let the printer manage the colours and then set your preferences in the printer driver.

Follow the steps below to print in greyscale via your printer's driver. This example will show the printer driver dialogue for an Epson 2880, running on Mac OS X 10.6.8 (Snow Leopard). Your dialogues will be somewhat different depending upon your operating system and printer manufacturer.

1 Specify the printer and page layout as you would for colour printing.

2 Set the Color Handling menu to Printer Manages Colors.

3 Click the Print Settings button.

4 Select Color Matching from the menu in the middle of the dialogue and make sure that EPSON Color Controls is selected.

5 Select Print Settings from the menu in the middle of the dialogue.

6 Select Grayscale from the Color menu and adjust Print Quality, etc. as needed.

7 Click Save to commit your changes and exit the dialogue.

8 Click Print to start the print job.

9 To retain your print settings for future printing, make sure you save your Photoshop file after printing.

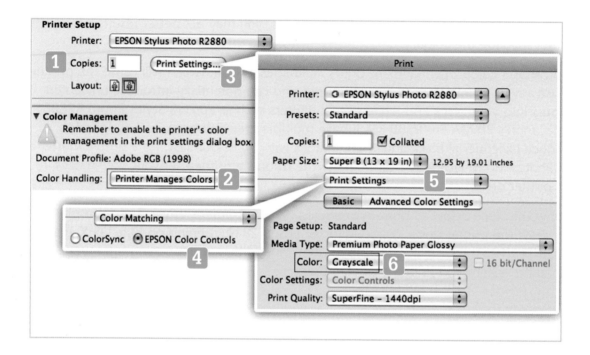

17 Save and output from Photoshop and Bridge

Introduction

This chapter is here because saving files is an often overlooked topic. It is worth stating explicitly up front that you should save your work repeatedly as you proceed. There is often a progression of files that gets created and saved along the way to your finished image. It might begin as a raw or JPEG file from your camera, or a TIFF file from your scanner. Once you bring the file into Photoshop, it's time to save your master file, which would typically be a Photoshop PSD file. From there, you might save a low-resolution JPEG to use as an email attachment, a high-resolution TIFF file for printing promotional cards at a service bureau, or even a separate PSD file that is optimised for printing on a large-scale ink-jet or giclée printer.

The last three items in this chapter could arguably have been put into Chapter 2, since they deal with Bridge. In the end, it seemed to make most sense to aggregate everything related to saving files into one place, with one exception – Camera Raw's Save Image feature is covered in Chapter 3 as part of the Camera Raw workflow.

Save a file as a Photoshop file

It's a good idea to save your master files in Photoshop format. If you distribute only JPEG and TIFF files, the .psd extension will tell you at a glance that a file is for your own internal work. When you save files in Photoshop, the dialogues are actually being presented by your operating system, so your screens may look different from what you see here. However, the general functionality is the same. You should check your operating system documentation or system help for additional information.

1 Choose File, Save As from the menu bar. The Save As dialogue will appear.

2 Enter a name for the file.

3 You can save the file into the current folder or select a new one. You may need to navigate the dialogue to another folder or create a new folder from within the dialogue.

4 Make sure Photoshop is selected in the Format menu.

5 If you're saving a master file with layers or alpha channels, make sure those items are ticked.

6 Always embed the Color Profile.

7 Optional: tick As a Copy.

8 Click Save.

? DID YOU KNOW?

If you combine lots of images, layers, smart objects, etc. into a single file, its size can exceed 2 GB and you will get a warning from Photoshop telling you the file could not be saved. In that case, choose Large Document Format from the Format menu instead of Photoshop. The file will be saved with a .psb extension instead of .psd. A PSB file can hold 4,000 terabytes. Photoshop always saves the contents of smart objects as PSB files.

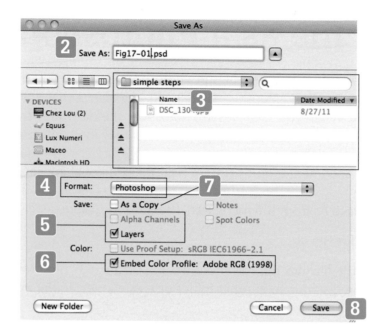

WHAT DOES THIS MEAN?

Save, Save As: the File, Save command is really a save and replace command. It deletes the previous version of a file and saves the new version in its place. File, Save As allows you to specify a new name and/or location for your file. If a file has never been saved before, the File, Save command does the same thing as File, Save As.

As a Copy: this option is useful for saving a file that works like a snapshot or a backup of your work in progress. Whenever you open a document in Photoshop, it becomes 'current'. When you choose File, Save, the current document gets saved and replaced. If you choose File, Save As, two things happen: a file with a new name is created, and that file becomes the new current document. You can override that behaviour by using File, Save As and ticking As a Copy. This option lets you save a copy of a file without changing the current document. For example, if you start working on a file called File01.psd and use File, Save As to create File02. psd, then File02 will be replaced each subsequent time you choose File, Save. If you tick As a Copy when you create File02.psd with File, Save As, then File01 will remain the current document and it will continue to be updated when you use File, Save. If you discover later on that you don't like some change that you made in File01 after you created File02, you can discard File01 and resume work on File02.

Save as TIFF

TIFF files are popular in part because, unlike Photoshop files, they are based on a published format (Adobe's DNG format is based on TIFF). As a result, most graphics software can read and write TIFF files and the format, along with PDF, has become a graphics industry standard. TIFF files are ideal for submitting your work to service bureaus for output. Some people use TIFFs interchangeably with PSD files, but there is no TIFF equivalent for the PSB file. One feature that distinguishes TIFFs is the ability to save them with loss-less LZW compression. The smaller compressed files take less time to transfer via the Web. The downside is that compressing and decompressing files can take time. Even though you can save TIFF files with layers and channels, they often cause problems for service bureaus, so in this section we'll look at how to save flat TIFF files.

To save a TIFF file, begin as you would for a PSD. Choose File, Save As from the menu bar and specify a name and location. Then do the following:

1. Select TIFF from the Format menu.

2. Untick Alpha Channels and Layers. This makes the file smaller and more portable. Photoshop will warn you that the file must be saved as a copy.

3. Photoshop may add the word 'copy' to your file name – change it, if you like.

4. Make sure you embed the colour profile.

5. Click Save. The TIFF Options dialogue will appear.

6. Optional: choose LZW for loss-less compression. (ZIP compression is not supported in some cases.)

7. You can ignore Pixel Order, Byte Order and Layer Compression.

8. Click OK.

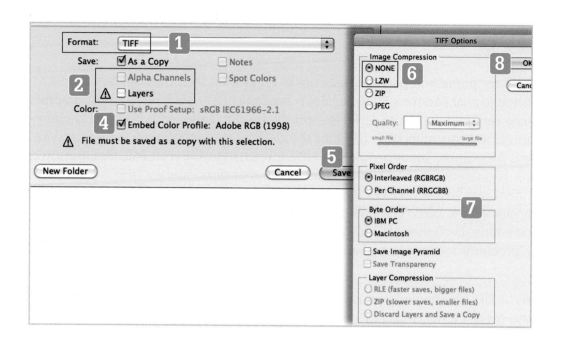

ALERT: JPEG compression makes files smaller by throwing away data and can dramatically degrade your image. If you want to use JPEG compression and you don't need layers, save the file as a JPEG instead. LZW or ZIP compression can't shrink your TIFF file as much as JPEG, but the files are identical to the originals when they are restored.

Save as JPEG

If you want to save one of your photos as a JPEG at the original resolution and with its original colour profile, you can easily do so with Save As. However, it's not the best way to save a JPEG if you need to upload it to a website or attach it to an email message, where you're likely to need to convert to sRGB and resample the image to make it smaller. You'll often do better to use Save for Web (covered in the next section) instead.

Regardless of the method you use to create a JPEG file, the biggest potential problem with the format is its characteristic compression artefacts. JPEG compression can make your files very small, but does so by degrading them drastically. Even at the highest quality level, JPEG compression discards lots of data, with a twist. There's very little visible difference between a quality setting of 10 and a quality setting of 12, but the difference in file size is more than double – a quality setting of 10 produces a file slightly less than 3 MB and a setting of 12 produces a file of just over 6 MB from a 10-megapixel image.

To save a file as a JPEG, select File, Save As from the menu and specify a name and location, just as with saving PSD files. Then do the following:

1. Select JPEG from the Format menu.

2. Make sure Embed Color Profile is ticked.

3. Click Save. The JPEG Options dialogue will appear.

4. Set the image quality.

5. Optional: toggle the preview tick box to see how your settings are affecting the image.

6. Set the Format Options as you like. Progressive files look different as they load.

7. Click OK.

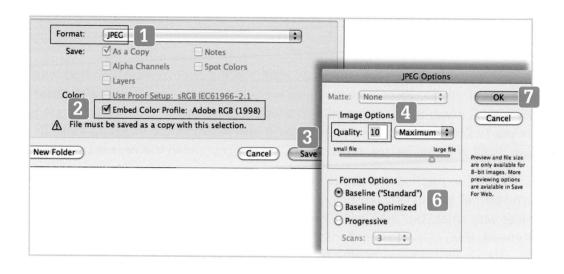

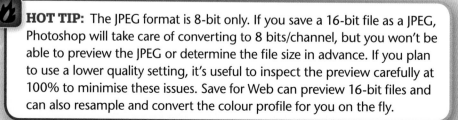

HOT TIP: The JPEG format is 8-bit only. If you save a 16-bit file as a JPEG, Photoshop will take care of converting to 8 bits/channel, but you won't be able to preview the JPEG or determine the file size in advance. If you plan to use a lower quality setting, it's useful to inspect the preview carefully at 100% to minimise these issues. Save for Web can preview 16-bit files and can also resample and convert the colour profile for you on the fly.

Use Save for Web

This command allows you to save images in any of the main formats that are used for web pages, email attachments, etc. It can also convert colour numbers to the more compatible sRGB colour space. Previews allow you to see how your settings will look and how big the files will be before saving. The quality scale runs from zero to 100. The quality 'sweet spot' is 80. Just as with the 12-point scale in Save As, there's very little visible difference between 80 and 100, but the file size more than doubles.

In CS6, the feature has been tuned so that you can use it with much larger files than before. In the past, you had to resample your files to a smaller size before using the command; now you can make lower-resolution files directly from the master files. To use the feature, select File, Save for Web from the menu bar. A dialogue will appear, then do the following:

1 Click the 2-up tab.

2 Choose JPEG from the file format menu.

3 Tick both Embed Color Profile and Convert to sRGB.

4 Select a level from the Compression Quality menu (medium, high, very high, etc.) or enter a number into the Quality field.

5 Optional: tick Progressive and/or Optimized as you like. If you're using a low Quality setting, you can apply blur to compensate for some artefacts.

6 Optional: select the amount of metadata you want to include.

7 Select an image size. If you are saving files for the Web or email attachments, 1000–1500 pixels on the long dimension is a good size.

- Optional: set the Quality menu to Bicubic instead of Bicubic Sharper for reduction or Bicubic Smoother for enlargement.

8 Click Save. A Save As dialogue will appear:

- Enter a name and select a location to save your file.
- Select Images Only and Default Settings from the Format and Settings menus at the bottom of the dialogue.

9 Click Save.

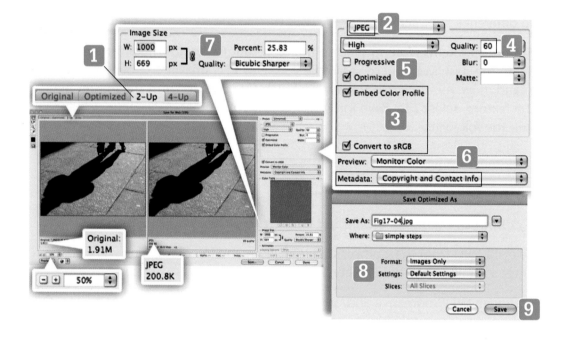

HOT TIP: Zoom in or out to evaluate the results as you're adjusting your settings. Zooming in to 200% or more will show JPEG artefacts more clearly, but generally you want to evaluate the image at 100%, since that's how other people are most likely to view it.

? DID YOU KNOW?

Other features of this dialogue include making animated GIF images and slicing images for use in advanced web design. See the help system or the Adobe website for more details.

Use the Export panel

The Export panel in Adobe Bridge contains a set of Output modules that offer a streamlined way to batch-export JPEG files. In addition to a Save to Hard Drive module, there are Output modules that can place files directly onto your Flickr, Facebook and Photoshop.com accounts. Their destination tabs contain site-specific login and gallery options.

All of the Output modules work the way the basic Save to Hard Drive module does, with minor variations. You drop a set of files onto it to create a queue, specify a destination, set image options, and click a button to run the batch. The module then creates the JPEGs and places them in the specified location. Because the Output module can process Raw files, it opens the possibility of a workflow that goes from camera to Web without touching Photoshop. You can also use Camera Raw to edit the Raw file, press Done and then drop it into the Export panel.

Click on the Export panel tab or choose Window, Export panel from the menu bar to display the panel. Details on using the Save to Hard Drive module are below:

1. Drag files to the module to queue them.

2. Click the triangle to the left of the icon to show the files in the queue.

3. Hover the cursor over the items in the queue for the option to view the file in Bridge or delete it from the queue.

4. Click the X on the Save to Hard Drive module to cancel the entire queue.

5. Click the arrow or double-click the module to edit the destination and image options.

6. In the Destination tab, set the location and specify how the new files should be named.

7. In the Image Options tab, set the file size, resample method, image quality and metadata to be applied.

8 Additional features not shown: you can add keywords as you export and you can save your settings as a pre-set from either tab.

9 Click Export to run the batch.

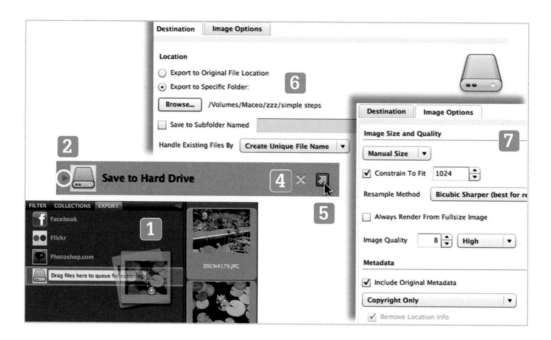

Create a web gallery with the Output Module

The Output Module workspace features a dedicated set of panels that you can use to build web galleries with ease. Bridge can upload the gallery directly to your web server. You can also save a copy to disk as an offline archive, and if you're comfortable editing web files, you can build a larger website by saving and linking several galleries together.

1. Gather the images you want to include in your gallery into a collection.

2. To switch to the Output Module, select Output from the Workspace Switcher or click on the Output icon in the header section and then click the Web Gallery button.

3. Drag thumbnails in the filmstrip to sequence them. If you select items in the filmstrip, only the selected images will be included in the gallery.

4. Select items from the Template and Style menus.

5. Fill in the Site Info and Create Gallery sections:
   - Make sure you enter a search engine-friendly Gallery Title. It will appear in the <title> tag of your gallery's pages.
   - Don't put punctuation or spaces into the Gallery Name field. It will be used to name a folder that Bridge will create when it saves the gallery to disk or uploads it to your web server.
   - If you plan to save the gallery to disk, you can type in a path or click Browse to select a location on your hard disk to save your gallery.
   - Use the Upload Location menu to load previously saved FTP settings. Once you enter your FTP server information, you can click the Save Preset Name icon to add an item to the menu. The trashcan icon deletes the current FTP location from the menu.
   - You don't have to enter FTP data if you plan to save your gallery to disk and use a standalone FTP tool.

WHAT DOES THIS MEAN?

FTP: stands for File Transfer Protocol. You use it to move large files more quickly than with other web protocols such as HTTP or email, and you'll use it to upload your gallery folder if you save it to disk and edit the HTML. If you are unsure about what FTP settings to use, talk to the people who manage the hosting of your website for information on how to log in and where to place your files.

6 Adjust attributes in the other sections as needed. Use the disclosure triangles to expand and collapse sections.

7 Optional: click the Save Style icon to add your settings to the Style menu.

8 Optional: click Preview in Browser to see what your gallery looks like with up to ten images.

9 Click Save to write a copy of your gallery to the hard drive and click Upload to send your gallery directly to the web server.

DID YOU KNOW?

The <title> tag of an HTML page contains the text that appears at the top of the web browser window. It is also what search engines pay the most attention to. Adding your name to the title makes it easier to find your pages when someone searches for your name.

HOT TIP: The Lightroom Flash Gallery and the Airtight templates use Flash and are not viewable on iPhones or iPads.

Make a PDF with the Output Module

In a fashion similar to creating websites, Bridge can combine a selection of images into a PDF file. You can even set the PDF so that it expands to full-screen mode and plays a slide show upon opening.

1 Gather the images you want to include in your PDF into a collection.

2 Select Output from the Workspace Switcher or click on the Output icon in the header section and then click the PDF icon. You can select a template from the menu as a starting point.

3 Drag thumbnails in the filmstrip to sequence them. If you select items in the filmstrip, only the selected images will be included in the PDF.

4 Set up the Document section, including paper size, orientation, image quality and optional passwords. Use the disclosure triangles to expand and collapse sections as required.

5 Use the controls in the Layout section of the panel to specify how images will be arranged.

6 Optional:
- If you want to review the PDF as soon as you save it, make sure that the box marked View PDF After Save is ticked.
- Use the Overlays section to add page numbering and filename captions.
- Add headers and footers.
- Use the Playback section to set Full Screen, automatic advance, looping and transitions.
- Use the Watermark section to add text or an image as a watermark.

7. To add the settings to the Template menu, click the icon next to the Template menu.

8. Click Refresh Preview to see what the first page will look like. The preview appears in a tab with the Preview panel.

9. Click Save and use the controls in the Save As dialogue to name your PDF and specify where it will be saved.

10. Click Save to generate the PDF. Click OK when Bridge confirms that the file was created.

 HOT TIP: Use Command | Ctrl + A to select all items in the filmstrip and Shift + Command | Ctrl + A to deselect all items in the filmstrip. Bridge will export all images in the filmstrip when none is selected.

Top 10 Photoshop CS6 Problems Solved

Problem 1: My keyboard shortcuts aren't working or Photoshop just beeps

When the text is highlighted or a blinking cursor appears inside a value box (e.g. a size field in the Options bar), that field is said to have 'focus'. This can interfere with keyboard shortcuts because the field soaks up the keystroke. Sometimes your typing may appear in the field, but at other times Photoshop will just beep. Hit Return | Enter to commit changes to the field or Esc to cancel and take the focus off the field. In some cases, you may need to reset the value of the field before you can commit it.

Similarly, you can't do anything else when editing text with the Type tool, and you have to OK or cancel dialogue boxes before you can go back to work in Photoshop.

1 When a field has focus, Photoshop will display a blinking vertical bar or a coloured highlight inside the field. In this example, the Opacity field will absorb any keystrokes.

2 The Opacity field is set and no longer has focus.

Problem 2: My cursor suddenly looks like a simple crosshair

If you're seeing a cursor that looks like a dot surrounded by four radiating lines, you could be in Precise Cursor mode, or perhaps you tapped the M key and activated the Marquee tool.

1 Turn off caps lock to exit Precise Cursor mode.

2 The Marquee tool cursor is similar. Check the Tools panel to make sure the right tool is selected.

3 If neither of these is the case, your brush size is probably very small. Tap the] (right square bracket) key repeatedly to make your brush larger. (Make sure you didn't turn caps lock on while trying step 1.)

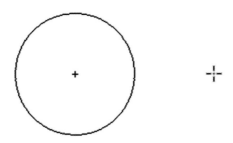

Problem 3: I keep losing my cursor

The mouse pointer is very small for a number of Photoshop's tools, so it's easy to have it 'submarine' and seemingly vanish.

1 Press the space bar to temporarily convert your current tool to the Hand tool.

2 If you still don't see it, wiggle the mouse a little. You should see the cursor waving back at you.

3 Move the cursor to where you want it, then release the space bar.

Problem 4: All my tools and panels just disappeared

When you hit the tab key in Photoshop the panels are hidden away. In Bridge, the right and left columns are hidden. This nearly undocumented feature can actually be very handy. It's just scary when you don't know about it.

1 Hit the tab key again to restore your tools and panels.

2 You can also hold down the Shift key and hit the tab key to hide or show just the right-hand and bottom panels in Photoshop.

Problem 5: I can't see any painting

When your painting is not showing up, there are several possibilities. This is not a comprehensive list, but it should get you started looking in the right places:

1 There is an active selection and you are attempting to paint outside the selection. Choose Select, Deselect from the menu to release the selection and try again.

2 Your edits are being applied to the wrong layer. An opaque layer is covering the active layer that is receiving your edits. You may have to step back in the History panel to undo the changes you made before selecting the intended layer and try again.

3 The active layer is inside a group that has its visibility switched off. Turn the visibility of the group back on to see your edits.

4 Your layer has a mask on it that is at least partially blacked out.

5 One last possibility is that you are in Quick Mask mode and painting with a white brush.

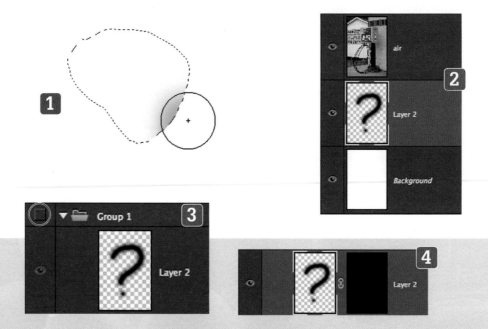

Problem 6: My cursor turned into a no symbol

Photoshop occasionally replaces the cursor with a circle-backslash sign to indicate that it can't apply a tool. Two cases where this happens are when you try to use the Brush tool on a layer that has its visibility turned off and when you try to apply the Brush tool to a smart object.

1 In the case of the smart object, you can add a blank layer above it or edit its contents by double-clicking its thumbnail.

2 In the case of the invisible layer, either select the layer you really meant to paint on, or turn the layer back on to make it editable.

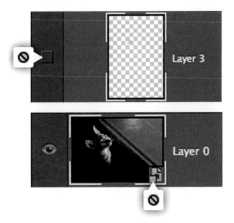

Problem 7: I'm getting a message about a missing colour profile

If you open a file without a colour profile, the colours you see may be completely wrong. To address the problem, Photoshop displays the Missing Profile dialogue so that you can assign a colour profile, so long as your colour settings have the Ask When Opening preference set for missing profiles. If you pick the wrong colour profile, your colours will still be wrong when the file opens, but as long as you don't also convert the document to the working space, that's not a problem because you can assign a different profile after you open it.

1 If you know the file was created in the Adobe RGB space, click the circle next to Assign working RGB to do so.

2 If the file came from the Web, it's a good guess that it is an sRGB image. Click the circle next to Assign profile to select it and choose sRGB from the profile menu.

3 If you are not certain about the right colour profile, do not tick the box to convert to working RGB. If you plan to convert to another colour space after you've finished editing it's also not a good idea to convert to the working space. Converting can shift colours and degrade your image.

4 Click OK to open the image.

5 If the colours look wrong, choose Edit, Assign Profile from the menu bar. In the Assign Profile dialogue, leave Preview ticked and click back and forth between Working RGB and Profile to see how the colours in your image change. Use the profile menu to compare results among Adobe RGB, sRGB and ProPhoto RGB. Click OK when you have found the best result.

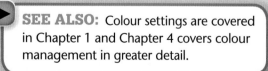

SEE ALSO: Colour settings are covered in Chapter 1 and Chapter 4 covers colour management in greater detail.

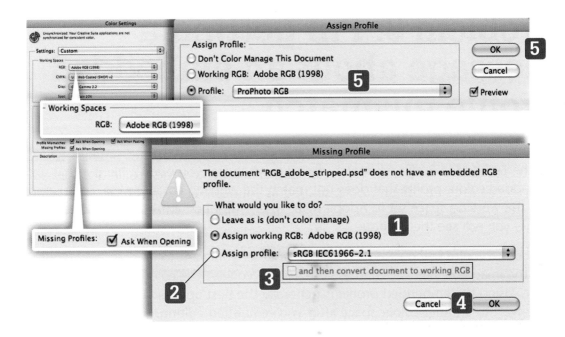

Problem 8: I'm getting a message about an embedded profile mismatch

If you tick the appropriate Ask When Opening option in your colour settings, you will see the Embedded Profile Mismatch dialogue whenever you open a file that has an embedded colour profile that does not match the working colour space. For example, with the working space set to Adobe RGB, when you open an sRGB or ProPhoto RGB image, you will see the dialogue.

The choice you're being asked to make is whether you want to work in the colour space that the image defines, or whether you want to convert the colours to the working space. Using the embedded profile is generally the best approach, especially if you plan to convert to another colour space after you've finished editing, since each time you convert colours, there is a chance you will get colour shifts.

If you do choose to convert the colours, there is less of a downside when you convert to a larger colour space, i.e. from sRGB to Adobe RGB or from Adobe RGB to ProPhoto RGB. If the image is in sRGB and you plan to adjust colours and tones, and make prints, there may be some benefit to upgrading the colour space to Adobe RGB. If you are opening a web file to adjust it and then post it back on the Web, there is no reason to convert from sRGB to Adobe RGB and back to sRGB.

Converting to a smaller colour space is more likely to degrade your image. The most problematic conversion would be to go from ProPhoto RGB to sRGB.

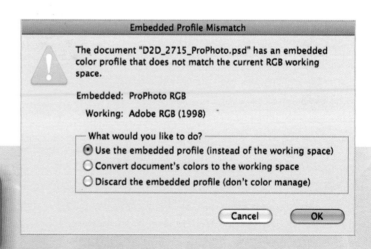

> **SEE ALSO:** See Chapter 4 for more on colour management and Chapter 1 for details on colour settings.